Cornish Folk & Fairy

A Collection of New and Traditional Stories

for Emma

Written by
Randle Hurley

Illustrated by
Sara Jenkins

Published by Plumstone Productions

ISBN 978-0-9562853-0-0

INTRODUCTION

We Cornish are blessed with a huge range of folk and fairy stories. In earlier times these were kept alive by wandering story tellers who moved from village to village, telling their 'drolls' at inns and other meeting places. Then the railways came, bringing peoples who demanded more sophisticated entertainments. Soon, we Cornish embraced sophistication and began to neglect our herritage.

In the latter half of the nineteenth century, enthusiasts began to collect the stories from the remaining droll tellers. Robert Hunt and William Bottrell were two collectors who published their collections and, although we should be grateful for their efforts, there were problems. For one thing, these academic gentlemen cut out all of the rude bits to avoid giving offence to their Victorian readers. Unfortunately they retained all the rambling and repetitive material and garnished the result with flowery, Victorian language. Before being thus recorded, the drolls existed in a continuous state of flux. They adapted to new tellers, to new audiences and to changes in society. Interesting happenings inspired new stories. Once written down, however, the old drolls became frozen for a century and a half. It is high time that they were set free once more to develop and grow into the twenty-first century.

In *'Cornish Folk and Fairy'* you will find new stories as well as old drolls re-told. The new tales have been inspired by life in West Cornwall, by the people we share it with and the landscape we enjoy. The style of story telling varies widely. Much of the language from the old version of *'Duffy and the Devil'* has been preserved but *'Agnes and Bolster'* is almost completely retold. The style of 'Gold and Silver' is taken from collections which my mother read to me as a child. I've used the dialect which we spoke in the fifties as well as some of my Grannie's expressions when writing tales like *'Bernice Penburthy'* and *'The Magic Potion'*. The dialect has been written with readability in mind rather than a slavish devotion to pronunciation. Pronunciation varied widely from village to village anyway. The Arthurian tale in *'The Watcher'* comes from *'Deep Down'* by R M Ballyntyne. The Golowan Festival in Penzance inspired *'Cap'n Trahare's Voyages'* and a surprising amount of *'Trouble at Treen'* is true.

At first I thought that the feel of some of the tales were a little 'darker' than children might enjoy. Some of Sara Jenkins' illustrations are certainly very hard hitting. I need not have worried because my eight year old grand daughter, a stern critic, demanded more after I read her one or two of the shorter tales and then insisted on hearing the lot. I now feel confident to offer this collection to those who read stories to children, children who read for themselves and adults interested in Cornish matters, folk stories and fairy tales.

Randle Hurley
June 2009

Contents

Bolster and Agnes

Giant Bolster was a villain. He beat his wife. He stole. He stole sheep, cows, pigs, horses and oxen. The only reason he didn't steal chickens was that they were too small and too feathery to bother with. He was not only a villain, he was huge and ugly, slovenly and smelly. Nevertheless Bolster loved.

Now, there's no reason at all why Bolster shouldn't love. For a giant, Bolster was a fine specimen. It would have gladdened the heart of any giantess to receive Bolster's attentions.

But
Bolster's love was Agnes. And not any old Agnes either. Bolster was besotted with the pious *Saint* Agnes, pillar of the early Celtic church in Cornwall.

Agnes **DID NOT** love Bolster.

The giant did everything he could think of to impress the saint. He left dead cows outside her cell every morning for a week. He blew away the mist whenever it might be troublesome to the saint. And he thought that she would be pleased if he piddled on her garden in the dry weather, to make her vegetables grow. But, most impressive of all, Bolster stood on the top of Carn Brea every evening and shouted at the top of his voice;

"I, Giant Bolster, LOVE Saint Agnes!"

Bolster's voice was so loud that soon, all the other saints in Cornwall learned about the affair and Agnes' reputation started to slip.

Agnes faced up to the hulking brute and told him. "You're s'posed to be a married man you are. I'm s'posed to be chaste. And not in the way you de mean neither. And if I was goin' to be chased then I'd find someone a bit better looking and a **LOT** better smelling than you to chase me, my hansome. G'won 'ome to your wife and you be a bit more Christian towards she. I've heard tell you de treat she some bad and that's a thing I can't abide in a man."

Bolster kept bellowing his love for Agnes from the Carn every evening. Before long, monks and nuns started to visit Agnes, trying to get her to mend her ways and to remember her vows of chastity and poverty. They didn't stay long. If they weren't disgusted by the ostentatious wealth of meat which the sister seemed to keep about the place, they were appalled by the stink of pools of piddle and the reek of bad breath from when Bolster blew the mist away. Bolster, once simply a nuisance, was becoming a major embarrassment. Something had to be done.

Agnes was desperate; desperate to be rid of Bolster; desperate to be free of the smell of piddle and halitosis; desperate to become a vegetarian. She formulated a plan, and not too Christian a plan either. She promised herself to Bolster **IF** he would do one small deed to prove his love for her beyond any doubt. Bolster was overjoyed. He said he would do anything.
"There is a small hole on the cliff near my home" Agnes told him "and you must fill it - with your blood". Bolster strode to the cliff, whipped out his knife, opened a vein and stuck his arm in the hole to bleed. He thought the hole would soon fill. Bolster was huge and he knew that he had gallons of blood. He kept his arm in the hole and waited. Blood gushed and soon Bolster started to feel faint but his love for Agnes was strong and he decided to bleed on.

The more he bled, the weaker he became until he was so exhausted that he was unable to withdraw his arm to staunch the flow. What Agnes knew, and Bolster did not, was that the hole had no bottom. Bolster poured out all his blood, all his love and eventually his life, into the sea.

Now - if you don't think that the saintly Agnes could play such a trick or if you think this is just a silly, made up story, you go to Chapel Porth, near Saint Agnes in Cornwall and you look. The cliffs are stained red with Bolster's blood to this very day.

An Pee Tregeer on All Hallows Eve

"Thees habn't got no ginger nor no saffron! Whateemean woman! Tis Hallen Eve and we're s'posed to have ferrins and saffron cake ready for the feastentide tomorrow. Do'st think I'll make do with fuggin, thou strumpet" Squire Trevaile was scarlet with rage at his housekeeper's news.
Peneope Tregeer twisted her towser in her hands while she endured the squire's furious gaze. "I'm some sorry, maister, but ee don't matter. I'll send Annie into St Just for some while I - "
"No you bleady wain't, An Pee!" bellowed the squire. "You're s'posed to be housekeeper and, seem me, the house is havin' to keep he's self. The maid shall stay here and the housekeeper, who was the one who forgot 'em, shall fetch the spices. And if she id'n careful, when she de come back she shall be the maid and the maid'll have took her place. And I aren't havin' none of that grey dust they de sell for ginger in St Just. I'dn no taste to un. You shall traipse all the way to Penzance and get fresh and I hope you de get bleady blisters commin' back!"

An Pee Tregeer on All Hallows Eve

"I shall go dreckly, maister, soon as - "
"I aren't havin no dreckleys!" bellowed Squire Trevaile.

Aunt Penelope, or An Pee as she was generally known, fled from the room, grabbed her hat and her shawl from the peg and a handful of coins from the housekeeping pot before scuttling out of the house and up the hill to take the Penzance road. An Pee knew better than to argue further. The squire and she had enjoyed many a battle and they were usually quickly forgotten, as long as the squire won.

"Cuss the old devil" said An Pee to herself. "Nine mile there and nine mile back! I shall be killed in this weather. I knaw, I shall call in on Jenny Trehair and see if she'll keep me company on the road to Penzance. Good company de shorten a journey as they de say."

Jenny Trahair was a friend of An Pee's and the wife of Tom Trahair, a fisherman who fished for brandy and tobacco over to France. Some say Jenny was a witch and that's why her man always had fair weather for his trips and never got caught by the revenue men. Some say that she was 'specially skilled at cussin' and there were even hints of her dealing with The Old One himself, to gain her ends.

Jenny's door was generally open all day, to facilitate trade and to spy the revenue men coming up the road but today it was shut tight. An Pee was about to lift the latch when she heard voices. She was a nosy old soul so she decided to peep through the latch hole before entering. She saw Jenny, holding a croggin and smearing some greenish salve from it onto Tom Trahair's eyes. An Pee waited a moment before knocking and opening the door. She found Jenny alone in the kitchen and noticed her concealing the croggin shell under a cloth on the stove. Jenny seemed a little confused but she recovered herself quickly and offered An Pee a drink.
"Will ee have a drop of rum what Tom have brought back from his last trip, An Pee? Ee idn' a bad drop but you shall have a splash of shrub in un if you've a mind to. Tidn' no less warming with the cordial and ee de make un taste handsome."

An Pee was glad to accept the offer and Jenny slipped out to the scullery to fetch the spirits and cordials. As soon as she had left the room, An Pee took the croggin from the stove and smeared a little of the salve it contained onto her left eye. There was a sensation of heat and discomfort as soon as the ointment touched her eyelid. This and the sound of Jenny returning prevented An Pee from anointing her right eye. Instead she hastily replaced the shell where she had found it and tried not to look guilty as Jenny entered.

"Here you are, An Pee" said Jenny, entering and leaving the door ajar. A moment later the door closed, seemingly of its own accord. Suddenly Tom Trahair appeared on the left hand side of the room which gave An Pee a considerable shock.
"My gar, Tom!" said An Pee. "You give me some fright. I didn' see ee there."
Tom seemed annoyed to have been noticed at all and gave her a black look before hastily leaving the cottage without a word to either of the women.

"I'm some sorry I cain't walk into Penzance with ee tonight, An Pee," said Jenny. I got too much to do for the feast yet and I got to be here should anybody want a drop of stuff for the festivities. But have a drop of Hollands gin before you go, to keep ee warm on the way and take some with ee for the way back."

An Pee was grateful to accept and she was soon on her way into Penzance. The sting in her anointed eye had faded and the fresh air made it water a little. The light was fading when she eventually neared Penzance but An Pee was surprised at how well she could see as she finished her journey. She made her way to the Market Place where she knew she could buy the spices she needed for the festival. She also took the opportunity to do a little shopping for herself at the stalls which clustered about the Market House. She greeted several people she knew as she wandered amongst the stalls and was surprised when she was given the same reply by all she met; "my soul, An Pee, I never saw ee there in the shadows." To the old woman, the evening was especially bright and everything in the market was as clear as crystal.

Suddenly, An Pee saw someone she knew well, darting from stall to stall. There was Tom Trahair, helping himself to the traders' goods and stuffing his pockets with his booty. Nobody seemed to notice Tom except An Pee and she approached him saying; "Whatever are ee doin' of Tom, steeling from these honest folks. Thee should'st be ashamed of theeself."

Tom turned on An Pee and looked at her closely. "Half in and half out, are ee An Pee? See me and be seen by they eh? Which eye can ee see me with?"

An Pee was astonished at his question and winked each eye

in turn. "Why, only with the left one" she exclaimed in amazement. Before she could regain her composure, Tom gave her a painful poke in her left eye and said with a threatening voice;

Cussed be thy prying eye.
And cussed be thee,
Thou peeping spy.

By the time An Pee had managed to open her eyes once more, Tom had vanished.
"Quick, stop un willee!" she cried to the stall holders. "You been robbed. Didn' ee see un?"
Several of the stall holders stared about them in amazement and only the nearest trader spoke to her. "Why there you are my beauty. I didn' see ee at first. What ee say about a robber my 'ansome?"
"Didn' ee see that feller filling he's pockets with your trade goods?" said An Pee. "He was standin' right in front of ee"
"Dossen't ee worry theeself, mother" said the trader. "You're the only soul who have been here for a good ten minutes. Market's nearly over. I should take yerself off home my 'ansome and dossen't ee stop at the inn on the way neither. I b'lieve you had enough already."

An Pee started to realise the power of the salve she had stolen. It improved your eyesight, but at the expense of everybody else's around you. The result was to make the wearer seem invisible to others. On her way back to Pendeen she started to notice things which had been mere rustles in the hedgerow on earlier trips home. Tonight she could see each tiny animal making the sounds, even though there was no more than a sliver of moon for light. Some startled her because she had never seen such creatures in her life before. She remembered the bottle of gin which Jenny Trahair had given her and she took a pull at this to steady her nerves as she went on her way.

When An Pee eventually arrived home, there was time for no more than an hours rest before breakfast time. The Squire was awake early for the feast and found An Pee in the kitchen, preparing the meal for the household.
"My soul and body! An Pee. You're lookin' as whisht as a 'I dunno what', you are" exclaimed the squire. "Have ee been up all night?"
"Near enough" said An Pee and the old woman told the squire the story of her journey and the strange happenings the previous day.

"Seem me, An Pee" said squire when she had finished "Tom was right. You been half in Piskeys realm and half out. One eye in this world and the other somewhere different! You make sure you de go to church and ask pardon for what you done, meddling with things you don't understand, and see what the parson can do about Tom Trahair's cussin of ee. Now, my dear, time to pitch to bakin' the ferrins.

"Oh my gar, Maister!" cried An Pee, a fearful look stealing across her face, "I was that mazed, I forgot the spices after all." The old lady saw the fury grow in the squire's face and, wisely, turned tail and fled from the room. The squire quivered with rage as he shouted after her; "Come back here, thou limb! Thees'll need more than the Parson when I de catch up with ee!"

Bernice Penberthy's Dancing Partner

Bernice Penberthy was a 'fine git maid'. Well, the 'git' bit was right enough. She had arms like legs and legs like tree trunks. The Cornish Wrestling Silver Cup could be hers for the asking if they'd only let women compete. Her hair was like a git furzy bush. She had feet so big it would be difficult to knock her over. Most impressive of all, however, was her voice. Now, it wasn't as deep as a bass nor yet as high as a tenor but powerful! And as for fine? Well you wouldn't say 'fine' as in a 'Fine Derby Tea Service', more like a 'fine git carthorse stallion'. Bernice shouldn't have wanted for a husband. She would have been a fine asset to any farm, being able to do the work of two men. She could call in the beasts for milking from three fields away. But then, you know men! They mostly don't know what they need. They only know what they want. And what they wanted was a lot less 'git' than Bernice had on offer.

She wasn't backward in coming forward with offers and she would bellow at any man she chanced to meet of a Friday;

"Right are ee, m'son!

Goin' dance t'night are ee?

I'm goin'. You ask me for a dance and I wain't turn ee down like all they other hoity toity maids de do."

These lucky fellows either didn't 'go dance' at all, or, if they did risk it, they stayed far away from Bernice all night. Poor Bernice was never asked to dance and she was even turned down when she approached other wall flowers like herself to say; 'if we made ourselves a couple then two fellas might come 'long and split us up, like'.

She tried expensive frocks from Lorna Lovell's shop in Penzance (special order, extra outsize) which never repaid the investment. She nearly set herself afire one week, using too much scent while standing close to the fire. If her mother hadn't been there to wrap her in a blanket she would have been a goner. It was a month before her moustache grew back

Bernice was close to despair. She'd had only one dance, with a short-sighted stranger, in all the time between Christmas and Easter. On the first Friday after Easter week, Bernice was on the way to the church hall as usual when she did a very foolish thing. Young maidens (nor nobody else for that matter) shouldn't say such things, but Bernice said, **OUT LOUD**;

> "If I don't get a man to dance with me tonight then I shall dance with the devil."

No good wishing her cake dough after saying that! How could Bernice have known that a strapping young devil, from the Pit of Hell itself, was lurking behind the blackberry bush? Up he popped, dressed smarter than you might imagine any devil would be dressed. Being young, he only had a shortish tail which was almost concealed beneath his fine frock coat.

"Goin' dance are ee maid?" asked the devil.
"What if I am?" replied Bernice, not wanting to seem too forward. "Anyhow," she thought to herself, "I wouldn't put it past they other maids to have put this feller up to it, for a laugh like."
"Come 'long of me and I shall dance with ee all night long, if thee'se a mind to" said the devil.
"You bleady mean it?" shouted Bernice.
"Right on, I de mean it!" shouted the devil.
"Leave us be off then. And don't leave no one try and hold us back" cried Bernice ecstatically.

The other maids giggled and nudged each other when Bernice arrived and 'went ladies' as was the custom. They laughed on the other side of their faces when, as she returned, her 'chap' strode over, grabbed Bernice and started dancing. Even the men stopped talking behind their hands to each other and stared at the 'fine git couple'. For three dances, they had the floor to themselves but gradually other couples joined in and the evening progressed more or less normally except that a wide space was always maintained around the 'fine git maid' and her feller.

The devil, having only recently been appointed to his job in the upper world, was unfamiliar with the charms of our local women. Looking around him in the hall, he soon realised that he had not chosen well but, devil or not, he remained a gentleman. He had said he would dance with Bernice 'all night' and gentlemen keep their words.

"Night then" said the devil as soon as the last waltz had ended.
"Aren't ee goin' to see me home?" asked Bernice, unwilling to allow the evening to end.
At her mother's door, the devil bowed and said "Night then."
"Aren't ee goin' to give me a kiss?" asked Bernice in a tone of voice that expected more than one.
The devil kissed her and then said "Night then" once more.

Now Bernice had very little training in these situations. She approached the situation logically. She had a man and the sensible thing would be to keep him. And that's exactly what she did. At first the devil just stood there with Bernice clinging on to him. When he tried walking away, she held on.

An hour before daybreak, and some miles away, the pair encountered a farm hand on his way to work.
"Look, Bernice" said the devil." Here's a feller who's a lot better lookin' than me. Why don't ee go off with he, maid?"
"Don't s'pose ee'd 'ave me" said Bernice, adding "I de like you just fine my 'ansome."
"Look at un", said the devil. "He got a 'ansome coat up to un to keep out the mornin' chill and I haven't got nothin' to warm ee with but me flimsy, go dancin', wear."
"That's true 'nuff" said Bernice.
"Hang on while I de have a word with un" said the devil.

Morveth stared suspiciously at the dancing devil and his attachment.
"Here, booy. Do us a favour and I'll grant ee a magic wish" whispered the devil to the farmhand.
"Gosson" said Morveth!
"What's that?" asked Bernice.
"Men's business" the devil answered her.
"To show ee what I can do" whispered the devil to Morveth "have a look in yer

coat pocket and see what wadn' there this morning."
"My Gar" said the farmhand, sarcastically. "Who'd have thought? Threepence! You're a wonder. No mistake."
"Times is a bit hard" explained the devil. "But that's only on account. That's nothin' to what I shall give ee if you can get this maid off my shoulder and lose her somewhere"
"Leave it to me" said Morveth.

"Let go of me, maid, and grab hold of he" said the devil to Bernice. "He's a pretty enough feller, good enough for you anyhow. He told me as how he de like the look of ee."
"Do uh now? I b'lieve I de like the look of ee too, and he's coat" mused Bernice. "This wind is a bit chilly idn' uh?" So saying, she let go of the devil and instantly siezed Morveth with an iron grip.
"Off you go, my bucca, and meet me back here when you've lost 'er" whispered the devil to Morveth.

Now Bernice made the mistake of holding fast to the coat and not to any portion of the man within. Cunning Morveth wriggled an arm out of a sleeve and soon, both arms were free.
"Ere! What ee wriggling for?" asked Bernice.
"I cain't help it" said Morveth "I'm thinking of what were goin' to be up to when I get you home" he added, loosening one coat button after another. They were fast approaching a hump backed bridge.
"Look, maid, there's the moon reflected in the water. Tha's good luck that is."
"Where?" asked Bernice.
"Lean over a bit more" said Morveth. "The reflection's under the bridge a bit."
Bernice leaned. Morveth wriggled, heaved, and ran. Bernice, clutching the coat but not its contents, tumbled over into deep water.

By the time Bernice surfaced, Morveth was running back to the devil to tell him the news.
"Quick, choose your wish" said the devil. "We got to clear out quick or one of us wain't never get rid of her ever again."
"I dunno" said Morveth. "I cain't think."
"Well you better cos she's on the bank. Quick as a flash, booy. She's comin' and she don't look too pleased."
"I dunno at all" said the farm hand.
"Well, I shall just have to owe yer wish to ee" said the devil. "When you know what you de want, come back here and whistle. I shall come up from

below and you can ask for your heart's desire. Now, quick, scat!"
Morveth took off, running like a long dog. Poor Bernice went off home to learn from her adventures and to plan for the next man who would be foolish enough to ask her to dance.

Taking a long way round, Morveth arrived at work to find the place in an uproar. It would seem that the witch Maureen Figgy (who was descended from Maggy Figgy herself and so had to be respected) had been slighted by the squire and had put a curse on the old man and his son. The boy was to die on the next new moon, and the father on the new moon after, and all because the squire had turned Maureen down as a daughter in law.

Morveth saw a way to advance his position on the farm from 'gash hand' to something more substantial.
"Squire, dosen't ee worry a fig" said Morveth. "I shall lift the curse and save ee, and the lad too, you see if I don't"
"If you do my handsome," said the squire, "then you shall have a plot of land for yer own and a passle of money to set ee up and I shall put in a word with the mother of that lill' maid down the lane that you de fancy. Although I was thinking of saving her for meself, but there you are! Now what ee goin' to do to save us? There id'n no pellor nor no wise woman in the whole of Cornwall that can raise Maureen Figgy's curse once she have spat upon the floor."

"I dunno . . . ."
"You bleady dunno!" screamed the squire and then, addressing his bailiff, "Chuck un out! And don't leave un come back here no more, the heathen, givin' we false hope and leavin' us despairin' still."
"I dunno, YET!" yelled Morveth. "But keep yer hair on, Squire. I shall have the solution to all yer woes in the mornin'."
"You bleady better!" warned the squire.

Back up to the bridge ran Morveth. He checked for Bernice but there was no sign of her. Before the whistle had left his lips, there, before him, stood the devil.
"I hope you made your mind up, cos its a sharp old climb up to grass from where I de live and I don't fancy making the trip every time you take it into your mind to purse yer lips" said the devil, a little tetchily. "What's yer wish?"

Morveth explained the difficulty and the devil pondered.
"I only said one wish" he complained "and here you are askin' me to save two lives. Tell ee what, best I can do is save the boy. On the evening of the new moon, I, your local devil, shall be sent up to claim his life and soul. When I

arrive, you step up smart and say 'You shan't take un' and 'begone back to where you come from' and I shall go, meek as a lamb, and tell The Old One that the boy repented at the last minute and I had to leave un behind. Now don't ee try it again cos ee's more than my job's worth if I disappoint the old man twice in two moons. Leave the old squire go where he's s'posed to."

Morveth pleaded, but the devil was unmoved.
"A deal's a deal" he said "and one is all you're gettin'."
Morveth was disappointed but he still had a month to think of a plan and save the squire, win his plot of land, his passel of cash and his 'maid down the lane.'
Time passed and, when the devil came to claim the boy, Morveth played out the scene like an actor on a stage. The squire was delighted.
"You only got one to save now Morveth, booy. I got every confidence in ee, now I seen what you're capable of. See ee here, next month."

The squire may have had "every confidence" but it didn't show in his face on the eve of the next new moon. The day faded and the sliver of moon in the darkening sky gave just enough light to show the devil approaching the squire's door. He'd just put his hand on the great iron knocker when up ran Morveth.

"You shain't take un" he panted. "He have repented and you shall go back below where you come from and leave the squire alone."
"What ee talkin' about?" hissed the devil. "I told ee I could save only one of 'em. Leave me alone to do my lawful business or I shall have to take you instead and you wain't like that I can tell ee."

The two fell into whispered but intense, conversation. It seemed touch and go for a while but suddenly a terrified look came over the devil's face and he disappeared as fast as he had done the month before.
"You're a marvel, sure enough, Morveth my son" said the relieved squire. "I thought I was a goner but I ought to have had more faith in ee booy."
"You don't know how close you came to your fate, Squire" said Morveth.
"But how did ee swing it booy?" asked the squire.
"I told un" said Morveth proudly "that the whole district had heard he was comin' to fetch the squire's soul today - including Bernice Penberthy!"

Madam Noy and Betty Trenoweth

Madam Noy of Pendre was a strong minded old gentlewoman who loved her hens. It's no wonder that she did for they were coppies, a magnificent and rare breed with fluffy tufts of feathers, or cops, on their heads. Madam Noy not only loved her coppies but she was very jealous of them. Friends begged for a few eggs to raise but they were always disappointed. Some offered money but these were rebuffed even more strongly. Even relatives were refused. Madam Noy wanted the pleasure of the handsome hens all to herself.

One May month morning, Betty Trenoweth prepared to try where all others had failed, to acquire some coppie's eggs. She dressed herself in her steeple crowned hat and her mantle and sat on a style near Madam Noy's barn and waited. Soon Madam Noy emerged from the barn carrying a bowl of corn with which to feed her chickens.

"Good morning to your honour" said Betty, rising from the style and curtseying to the gentlewoman. "Dear me, how well your honour is looking. Seem me you're gettin' younger every time I de see ee. And what handsome hens and ducks and geese you got. The finest in the Parish I de believe."

"Gosson with ee, Betty Trenoweth" was all Madam Noy would reply.

"Do ee knaw, Madam dear, that I got an old clucken hen at home that I should dearly love to put to set" said Betty "and the eggs that I should like best for she, would be some of your coppie's eggs. I wondered if you might spare me a dozen, Madam Noy?"

"I thought you might" said Madam Noy mockingly "but I

haven't got none of they to spare nor no others neither. You de knaw very well that I always refuse friends and even kin folk whenever they make so bold as to ask. Whatever made ee think I should give any to the likes of you?"

Betty Trenoweth, who was all salutations and smiles at first, soured like the milk when thunder threatens. A stormy, steely edge came into her voice as she told Madam Noy "I don't give a cuss what you de say to your kin, but if you wain't sell me the eggs then you shall wish your cake dough."

"Git off home with ee, old bitch!" said the lady, allowing her rage to rise to counter the change in Betty's demeanour. "What business have ee got, covetin' all thee couldst spy with thy evil eye? Begone, or I'll set the dogs on ee and throw fire over ee. I aren't afraid of thy witchcraft."

"I am on the Church road to the town place, where I've a right to be and where I shall stop so long as I de like, in spite of you and all your lawyers" shrieked Betty. Madam Noy was well known in St Buryan for her love of the law and the bullying way she used her riches to drag her neighbours into court where few could afford to go.

"I shain't need no lawyers to deal with flea bites of trouble like you" cried Madam Noy and she stooped down and picked up a stone and let fly at Betty. The stone hit home and made Betty's jaws rattle. She limped back to the stile and climbed onto the topmost step so that she might look down on Madam Noy. At this height, wearing her steeple crowned hat and a mask of fury on her face, Betty was well placed to terrify her adversary. At first she kept her voice low and mumbled "now may the Devil help me, and by all that's evil here, I will curse thee to my heart's content."

Slowly Betty raised her arm and pointed a finger at Madam Noy. Next she raised her voice from its mumble to let her curse lose.

Madam Noy and Betty Trenoweth

"Mary Noy, thou ugly, old and spiteful plague,
I give you the colic, the palsy and the ague.
All thy hens' eggs from this day shall addle.
All thy birds shall have the pip and die with the straddle.
And before nine moons have come and gone,
Of all thy coppies there shan't live one.
Thy arm and thy hand that cast that stone
Shall wither and waste to skin and bone."

Madam Noy had heard many rumours about Betty Trenoweth and she was suddenly convinced that they were all true and that she was, indeed, a witch. Her face whitened and the old lady turned and fled home. For more than a week she kept to her house, not even stirring to feed her beloved hens. Those which managed to survive on what they could scratch from the ground were soon taken by foxes. When Madam Noy eventually dared to venture into the open air she found that the first part of Betty's curse had come true. All the coppies were dead.

Convinced of the power of Betty's curse, Madam Noy's attention turned to her right hand and arm. She so protected the limb that it grew thin and wasted from lack of use. In a few short months it had come to resemble a claw more than a human hand and the old lady never regained the use of it.

So, was Betty Trenoweth a witch? We shall see.

Piskey Threshing

Now, my 'ansomes, you remember me tellin' of ee all about An Pee Trageer who was sent to Penzance for ginger and saffron on All Hallen Eve? Well some people de tell that story a bit different from me. I s'pose I better tell ee the other side of the tale or you'll be sayin' as how I don't give ee good measure.

Lots of these here stories I'm a tellin' to ee, they weren't never wrote down 'til recent times. In the old days, before schoolin' and book learnin' got goin', nobody much could read or write. Stories, or drolls as they used to be known, had to be learned by heart and, of course, not everybody could do it. They who could learn the tales used to travel from place to place to recite them and were well looked after wherever they went. Everyone in the district would come flocking when a droll teller turned up. Droll telling was one of the most important sources of entertainment in they days.

Now then, what de ee think might happen after a hundred years or so? A story would be learned by you, listening to somebody else tellin' of it. And perhaps you might remember it a bit different from that somebody else. If you was a bit inventive, you might add a little bit here and there. If a story contained a detail which showed your family up in a bad light, maybe you would leave that bit out or you might change the name. If you was a bit wicked you might put in some rude bits to spice things up. There were all sorts of ways to make the old drolls change and change they did. For one thing they got longer and longer!

In the reign of Good Queen Victoria, two fellas made it their business to record the old drolls which were fast going out of fashion. William Bottrell and Robert Hunt thought it would be a real shame if the old tales disappeared so they wandered around, seekin' out the remaining droll tellers and writin' down their stories to put them in books. Now, people in Victorian days were very polite and so they left out all the rude bits and you probably think that that's a good job! What you wouldn't like so much was the way they used flowery language and repeated theirselves somethin' aweful. And they did tend to go on a bit. That's why I been and retold the old drolls to make them a bit more suitable for people these days. I hope you think I done a good job. I done me best anyhow.

Now then, where was I to? Oh ess, Tom Trageer had poked An Pee in the eye and cussed her. What happened then was ... by the time An Pee had managed to open her eye once more she slowly began to realise the power of the salve she had stolen. It improved your eyesight, but at the expense of everybody else's around you. The result was to make the wearer seem invisible to others. On her way back to Pendeen she started to notice things which had been mere rustles in the hedgerow on earlier trips home. Tonight she could see each tiny animal making the sounds, even though there was no more than a sliver of moon for light. Some of the sights startled her. She had never seen such creatures in her life before. She remembered the bottle of gin which Jenny Trahair had given her and she took a pull at this to steady her nerves and went on her way.

An Pee trudged wearily on towards Pendeen, getting more exhausted at every step. The dozen or more miles she had walked, the excitement of the market, her aching eye and the rum and gin she had drunk that day, all these had wearied her sorely and she craved rest. When she came to Boslow she decided to creep into the barn there and sleep a while. She could still be up and away home before the Squire woke the following morning.

As she placed her hand on the latch of the barn door she heard, coming from inside, the sound of grain being threshed.
"My gar! Who on Earth can be threshing at this time of night?" thought An Pee and peered through the crack where the barn doors met. It was entirely dark inside but, to her astonishment, An Pee could see light streaming under the left hand door. The old woman then applied her left eye to the gap and, immediately, could see the interior of the barn perfectly lit. And what she saw inside was even more amazing than any of the other happenings on that extraordinary day. Quietly as a mouse, she lifted the latch and opened the door a crack so that she could see the drama being played out in the barn more clearly.

The barn was lit with tiny lanterns hung on all the beams. The threshing was being done by a ragged creature, something *like* a man but even more *unlike* one! He was about half normal height but his shoulders were as broad as the squire's. Broadest of all was the creature's mouth which stretched from ear to ear, giving him the appearance of a frog, but a frog with a long, pointed snout of a nose. His legs looked too spindly to hold him up and his arms were even thinner but he worked with a will at the threshing and never stopped. Sheaves were brought to him by even smaller men who also took away the straw and collected up the grain. In this way, Piskey, for that was he who stood in the middle of the barn, could go about his work without having to break his rhythm.

Piskey worked so vigorously that clouds of dust rose from the threshing floor and, as she watched, they reached Piskey's nose and started him sneezing. Being a kindly soul, An Pee called out "God bless ee, little man" before she could stop herself. Instantly the lights were put out, a handful of dust was thrown in An Pee's face to blind her and Piskey and his helpers scuttled away. When An Pee could see again through her streaming eyes, the barn was in darkness.

At first she thought she might rest in the barn now that it was empty. Then she remembered tales of the spite shown by the little people towards those that spy on them and decided to make haste for home and the safety of the Squire's house.

Some say that, on her way home, An Pee was 'piskey led' when she tried to cross the Gump. There she saw further fairy folk who played tricks upon her and lead her further and further out of her way until she was hopelessly lost. They say that An Pee remembered, just in time, that the best way to avoid being Pisky Led was to turn some of your garments inside out. This she did and thus saved herself from further torment and, eventually made her way back home, to Squire Trevaile's manor.

Duffy and the Devil

Squire Lovell was an enthusiastic huntsman. His farms and lands were all let to good tenants who were kept well up to the mark by his bailiff. The old man was thus able to indulge his passion for sport most days of the week. Returning from hunting one day he passed Jenny Chygwin's door and, as he needed some help with the apple harvest, stopped to knock. Duffy Chygwin and her stepmother were fighting and Jenny was chasing the girl round the kitchen and beating her with her skirt.

"I'll break every bone in her body" cried Jenny. "The idle slut is too busy courseying, or couranting with the boys all day, to boil porridge, spin or knit."

"Don't believe her, squire" said Duffy. " 'Tis me that does all the work while she, the old baggage, is drunk from morning to night. My knitting and spinning is the best in Churchtown. They stockin's you got on are nothin' to what I could knit for ee."

"Stop beating the maid and raising so much dust from your old gown, Jenny, or you'll have me sneezing" said the Squire. "And Duffy," he added, "if you can spin and knit so fitty, come to Trove and help old Joan. She's blind in one eye and almost so in the other. No wonder my breeches and stockin's are in such a state."

The girl's stepmother was glad to be rid of the lazy maid. "Go off with the old bucca if thee's a mind to and good riddance to ee" she cried and slammed the cottage door. Without hesitation, Duffy jumped up behind the old man and rode off to a new life in Trove.

"Joan!" bellowed the squire when they reached Trove Manor, "here's Duffy Chygwin, come to help ee knit and spin. Give her some bread, cheese and beer. I'll be home when I find more help for the orchard."
"I'm glad to see you, Duffy" said the old housekeeper as the squire rode away. "I've sorely needed help, ever since Tom Chynance put out the sight of my eye. You needn't eat bread and cheese though. Dinner will be ready soon. Go up to the loft whenever you please and card wool ready for spinning this afternoon."

"Cuss the carding and the spinning" muttered Duffy to herself, seated later in front of a pile of wool in the dusty loft. "What shall I do now the wool is carded? I can neither spin nor knit and the Devil take such work from me." Now, this was a very dangerous thing to say as many have found to their cost. Duffy Chygwin was the prettiest maid in Buryan Church Town by far and it so happened that a young devil had lusted after her for some while.

The very next time Duffy looked up from the wool, there in front of her stood a handsome gentleman, the forked tip of his tail just visible beneath the tail of his jacket.

"Here I am, at your call," said the bucca boo with a bow, "ready to do any work, and for very little pay. Only agree to go with me, at the end of three years and I shall do all the spinning, knitting and anything else you may wish of me during that time. Even then, if you can tell me my name at three times of asking, you may stay if you wish."
"I don't mind much" said Duffy. "Anything for a change! What did you say your name was?"
"You have only to prick your arm, draw blood and sign our agreement" said the devil, producing a pin from the collar of his jacket and a paper from the pocket.
"My word is as good as my mark" said Duffy. "Spin and knit for me and, while you do, I shall coursey in the orchard and dance at the mill. Just keep the door bolted while I'm away, so none know 'tis you that's doing the work."

Old Joan, hearing the rumble of the turn every day, believed Duffy to be working hard. Duffy passed her time pleasantly at Trove Mill, where women of all classes met to grind their grain. Some would work while others told stories, sang or danced on the green. As time wore on, a friendship grew between the maid and Betty Chymellan who worked the mill. Betty, cunning witch that she was, saw at once that the stocking which Duffy pretended to be knitting, always had a stitch down and the work never grew.

On the first evening, Duffy returned to hear the devil spinning. She looked through the latch hole of the loft door to watch and see if she could learn something. The bucca boo seemed to spin straight from the fleece, without bothering to card the wool. In spite of this, his thread was amazingly fine and perfectly even. The wool appeared to wind itself and the balls rolled themselves into a neat pile at his feet. And all of this was accomplished at such speed that it was difficult to follow the motion of the devil's hands.

Duffy knocked gently and seemed to hear herself ask 'who's there' but it was only the devil, pretending to be Duffy, working hard. When she announced herself, he opened the door saying; "How are you, my dear? I've been hard at work. See what I've spun already" He pointed to the balls of wool and the many skeins hanging from the walls. "When you come back tomorrow there will be stockings for you as well as for the Squire. See if they don't fit both of ee perfectly. But for now, goodnight!" And the devil disappeared, taking with him all the yarn he had spun and leaving nothing behind except a slight smell of brimstone.

The next evening, the Bucca Boo handed her six pairs of stockings as strong as broadcloth but as fine as silk.
"Excuse me, my dear," he said with a bow, "but I must be away before Buryan bells are rung."
"I wish ee well till I see ee again Mr - er - What-Shall-I-Call-Ee?"
"You may call me Cap'n" said the cunning Bucca, disappearing again, this time with a gentle roll of thunder.

On Sunday morning, while Squire Lovell was putting on his velvet suit to ride to church, Duffy presented him with a pair of stockings. "You see, master, I haven't been idle. I've spun wool and knitted you a pair of stockings in three days, and the work so fine too."
Squire Lovell was so delighted at the fit and the quality of the knitting that he kissed Duffy, over and over. When he reached church, all the congregation admired the stockings. The ladies asked where they could buy such work for themselves as the stockings were fit for a king. The following Sunday, Buryan church was packed tight. Word of Squire Lovell's stockings had spread and old and young alike wanted to feel his legs, declaring they 'couldn't appreciate the work just by looking.' For weeks, Buryan Sundays were like feasten tide.

One evening, Duffy returned from the mill, went up to the loft and dismissed the devil from his work before going into the kitchen as usual. There she found Joan, seated in the inglenook, groaning loudly.
"Oh Duffy, dear, I got cramps in me belly and wind enough to make me headlight. Help me up over stairs to bed. Can you give maister his supper?"
When Duffy returned to the kitchen, she found that her admirer, Huey Lenine had arrived.
"What cheer, Duffy?" called Huey. "Now, thee cus'nt say that the lanes are longer than my love when I'm come to see ee in all this whisht, wild weather."
"Sit by the fire, my handsome, and dry thyself" said Duffy. He did as he was bid and they sat in silence in the inglenook for a long while.
"Why dosn't ee speak to me, Huey?" Duffy asked.
"What shall I say, love?" he replied.
"Say thou does't love me for sure" the maid prompted him.
"So I do" said the lad.
"That's a dear" said Duffy, pleased with his admission. "Brave pretty waistcoat you got up to ee then, Huey."
"Cost pretty money too" he replied.
"What did a cost then?" Duffy asked him.
"Two and twenty pence, buttons and all" he told her, hoping she would be impressed by his easy way with his money.
"Take care of un then" Duffy advised him.
"So I will" said Huey.
"That's a dear" said his sweetheart"
After another long pause during which Huey gathered his courage, he spoke again.
"I'm thinkin' we will get married next turfey season if thee west."
"I'll be married to ee any day, though thou art no beauty, to be sure" Duffy answered him. "Thy face is as rough as Morva Downs that were ploughed and never harrowed. But I'll have thee for all that, and fill up with putty all the pock mark pits and seams; then paint them over and make thee as pretty as a new wheelbarrow."

Before Huey could move closer to his love, the squire's dogs were heard outside. "Maister will be here in a minute," said Duffy, "crawl in the oven. A little more baking will make thee no worse".
Huey did as he was bid and just in time too.
"Joan!" roared the squire, "take up the pie, if its ready or raw. I'm as hungry as a hound."
"Master, I shall give ee yer supper" said Duffy. "Old Joan has gone to bed with cramps and wind. Here's your pie, baking on the hearth."
"Duffy, my dear," said the squire, taking a mouthful of pie, "these are the very best stockings that I ever had in my life. I've been hunting all day over moor, through bog, furze,

thorns and brambles. There isn't a scratch on my legs and they're bone dry."
"I may as well tell ee, master" announced Duffy "that I shain't be knittin' for ee much more because Huey Lenine and I have been courtin'. We're thinkin' to get married before winter and then I shall have a man of my own to work for."

Scarlet anger coloured the squire's face. "Huey Lenine! I'll flay him alive if he shows his face near this place. Why the devil would a young skit like thee take it into her head to get married? Now listen here to reason a minute. Give up courtin' Huey Lenine and I'll give ee silks and satins fine."
"I could never marry an old man like you" cried Duffy. "I need a lusty lad to keep me happy, one with all his teeth, who will louster all the day for his maister and half the night time for me."
"Huey Lenine will louster all his days for he cain't schemie to save he's life" argued the squire. "The night shift will soon slacken off with all the work with threshal and showel he shall have to do to keep ee. And when I say 'keep ee', you shall soon see the difference between 'kept by Huey Lenine' and 'kept by Squire Lovell'."
"But Huey is young and pretty and thou, Squire, why the end of thy nose is as blue as a bluebottle."
"Huey Lenine is ten year older than you, maid" retorted the squire "and the pox hasn't made him handsomer. You take ee and you shall leave behind presses full of silken gowns, all 'broidered in gold, and a chest of jewels and rings as thee dids't never behold."
"'Tis true my Huey is no beauty but I have to fight him off or I'd be crying at Christmas for April fooling."

The squire, believing action was called for to press his advantage, grabbed Duffy and began hugging and kissing her.
"You shain't find me feeble my lovely" cajoled Squire Lovell. "I might be near sixty but you'll find me stronger than many a man of twenty. Thou shalt ride to church behind me and I'll wager that you'll look finer than Dame Pender or Madam Trezillian."
"Keep your distance and stop of your hugging" cried Duffy. "Even if I do agree to take ee, you shall kiss me no more till you take me to church. Now look! The sand in the glass is all down and your pie is burned black. So off to the hall, and take your supper."

Duffy rose, took up the pie and pushed the squire into the hall to eat his ruined meal. She returned to see Huey crawling out of the oven. Duffy grabbed her sweetheart and bundled him out of thc house.

"Take thyself off, Huey Levine" she cried after him "and don't ee come back no more. I would have married ee but why should I take a piejack like thee when I can have a squire of high degree."

The next day the news had reached the mill early. All the gossips agreed that Duffy would behave as all other beggars put on horseback.
"I got a feelin'" said one good woman "that she'll soon wish her old husband dead. I should far prefer to be a young man's slave, than an old man's treasure, to be admired on the mantle and never taken down for good use."

Duffy was wed to her squire and became a grand lady, dressed in grand attire. She kept the bucca boo at his work and filled every chest and press with stockings, blankets, yarn and homespun. Soon the squire was clad from top to toe in devil's raiment. He continued to hunt from dawn to dusk while Duffy spent her time with Betty at the mill. The Cap'n worked in the loft and Joan still believed that the rumbling from above was Duffy hard at work.

At the mill, Duffy continued to knit the same old stocking, never finishing it but dropping more stitches. Before many weeks of married life had passed, Duffy complained to Betty about Squire Lovell's lack of attention to his husbandly duties.
"Bide yer time, my lovely" advised Betty "and feather yer nest. The squire wain't last for ever and you might find yerself a younger successor to un 'fore long."

Time passed and Duffy gave little thought to the problem of the bucca boo's name. Indeed, the devil seemed so obliging that she thought she might as well go with him when the time came, as stay with old Squire Lovell. But, when she wandered through Trove bowers, with apple trees bowed down with fruit, she had some misgivings, lest her next abode be much less pleasant . Besides, the devil might be, as most men, attentive during courtship but quite otherwise when he had her in his power. Again Duffy made her troubles known to Betty. The miller had already guessed that Duffy might be dealing with a devil. The squire's stockings were none of her work if the stocking on Duffy's kneedles signified anything.
"I aren't surprised, Duffy, my dear" she said after a few minutes twirling her thumbs. "Cheer up. I wouldn't like for ee to be taken before me. Your young devil is but a green one and I believe I've found a way to save ee. Make sure that the squire goes hare hunting at sunset tomorrow. Soon as he's gone, bring me a blackjack of your oldest and strongest ale. When your husband returns, take special note of what he says. Go home now, don't ask me no questions but be sure and do exactly as I've told ee."

The next day Duffy ate nothing for breakfast and moped about the house all day. She refused all that was set before her at dinner. The squire was moved to ask her why she seemed so out of sorts.
"Don't I do as much to comfort ee as any man? You don't appear to have much appetite, my honey. What would you like to eat?"
"I could just pick the head of a hare" Duffy replied. "You're so busy with the

harvest that you haven't been out hunting for weeks. I'm longing for a hare pie. I fear that if I don't get one then the consequences for the babe unborn would be dreadful."
"Harvest is late" he told her angrily "and we still have much corn to get in. Besides, its full time to pick the apples for cider making. I'd do my best to catch a hare to please ee but that chield has been coming for two years now and that story isn't enough to keep me from my corn or my apples."
"You hardhearted, unbelieving wretch" his wife retorted. "Don't you know that innocent virgins are often deceived with false hopes when they are first wed. Would you have our child disfigured for the sake of what little use you are to the men at harvest time? Do ee want the chield to have a face like a hare for the want of satisfying my fancy? Be a dear and stay my longing. After croust will be soon enough for ee to start. Then we may have hare pie tomorrow."

As soon as the squire had left, Duffy drew a gallon of the oldest beer into a leathern jack and took it to the mill. Betty tried it and said it would do very well but didn't explain what for. Duffy was sent home with orders to keep the bucca boo busy until after dark and then wait up to hear what her husband would say when he returned from hunting.

When it was nearly night, Betty turned the water from the mill wheel, donned her steeple crowned hat and red cloak, fastened the jack of beer to her girth and set out. She went along the bottom between Trove and Boleigh until she reached the fuggo hole where she disappeared. Duffy waited up for hours, sitting in the chimney corner, tending to a pie on the hearth that it might be hot for the squire's supper. At midnight Squire Lovell returned in a state of great excitement, laughing, singing snatches of song and capering about the kitchen. Poor Duffy could make neither head nor tail of what he said. Eventually, tired out, the squire called for a flagon of cider which he drained and calmed himself a little. When his wife asked him if he had caught a hare he started laughing again.
"I've seen queer sights tonight" he told her. "And that damned hare, most fine animal as ever was chased, we coursed her for miles but couldn't catch her." And then he burst out singing again.

'Tomorrow, my fair lady
You shall ride along with me
Over land and over sea
Through the air and far away!'

Oh! the funny devil, how he tossed up his heels and tail when he danced and sang. I've forgotten the rest but fill the flagon again and give me my supper and I'll begin at the beginning and tell ee all about the strange things I've seen tonight. I wish you'd been there, Duffy my dear, it would have made ee screech, laughin'."

After he had eaten and drunk, Squire Lovell told his tale more calmly.
"We searched all night, down to Lamorna without success. It was dark when we turned for home, with only starlight to see by. Suddenly, near the old fuggo hole at Grambler Grove, up popped a hare. She was a fine beast and we chased her for miles. She kept just ahead of the dogs, teasing them seemingly, but they couldn't catch her until we found ourselves once more in Grambler Grove. Now I know that it's true what they say about that place. Witches do meet there in the fuggo, to deal with the devil. I believe that the hare which led us such a dance was one of 'em. The dogs skulked back but I pressed on to see what I could. There were lots of 'em, young witches as well as old, sitting round a fire they had made. By the firelight, who do ee think I could see but our old Betty of the mill. By her side sat a strappin' young feller who you might not take for a devil at all but for the company he was keeping. Now and again old Bet held a flagon to his lips and he seemed to like the liquor she was feeding him. I said to meself, 'I don't much dislike ee, devil or no, as thou art so honest as to drink hearty.' He seemed to be drunk by the way he capered round the fire with the witches, hand in hand. Then he drained the jack and sang a tune I've never heard before. The words he sang were, so far as I recall,

I did knit and I did spin
For three years to the day.
Tomorrow she shall ride with me
Over land and over sea
Far away, far away
For she can never ever know
My name is Tarraway

And the witches took up the chorus;

By night and day
We dance and play
With noble Captain Tarraway.

I thought the words odd for a dancing tune but then, witches and devils do strange things. They danced and sang the song over and over, pulling each other through the fire and yet they weren't even singed, the bitches. The devil spun round and round so fast that I felt meself getting caught up in the excitement and finally cried out; 'Hurrah, my merry Devil and witches all.'
In an instant all was dark and the music stopped. A blast of wind swept away the fire and the ashes nearly blinded me. When I could see again, all had vanished and I was outside the fuggo hole once more."

The squire asked Duffy for another flagon of cider and drank it before rolling off the bench, onto the floor and going to sleep. Duffy covered him with a blanket and tucked some rushes from the floor under his head and left him there, where he often slept after hunting. As she left the kitchen she heard him drunkenly muttering;

"Tomorrow she shall ride with me
Over land and over sea
Far away, far away
For she can never ever know
My name is Tarraway"

The next evening the Squire went off hunting again, looking once more to see the places he visited on the previous night. Duffy, who had kept downstairs all day, went up to the guest room to fetch a garment from the press. As she turned to leave the room, the bucca boo stood in the doorway. He was dressed more finely than ever before, in a broad-brimmed, plumed hat and a buff coat of leather with wide skirts. The Devil approached, doffing his hat saying;
"Know, lady, that the time of my engagement is passed and a few hours over. I hope you have no reluctance to fulfil your part of the agreement."
"Indeed, no" Duffy answered. "I can't say that I have much objection, for you are a very well behaved and well meaning devil. During the three years of our acquaintance, you have given me no cause to complain of your behaviour. Yet, I'd like to know what sort of country yours is. I fear it might be very hot for you seem to be burnt very dark."
"You wouldn't be much wiser if I were to tell ee" said the bucca. You having seen so little of the world, there would be great difficulty making ee understand. Besides, I'm strong and healthy enough and not so dark, under my clothes" he added with a wink. "Anyway, even if you were burnt so black as myself then I should love thee just the same."
"I can't quite make up my mind though" said Duffy teasingly. "No doubt you would make a better husband than Squire Lovell who, if he isn't drunk, snores all night with his face to the wall. And if I went, how would you convey me to your far country?"
"I have brought to Grambler Grove, a steed which will go over land or sea, even fly in the air. Now get ready my dear for my horse don't care to be left alone. He may paw the ground and make the country tremble, yet he is as gentle as a lamb when he is mounted. Come as you are, there is no time for delay."
"If you please, I should like to stay in Trove a little longer" declared Duffy.
"No nonsense!" said the bucca sharply. "I have been true to my word as any gentleman should and I trust you will abide by our bargain. My proper title has been so long unused that I doubt you will know it. I am little known hereabouts and yet, my love, for form's sake, I'll ask ee the three times. Besides I'm curious to know what sort of a guess you will make at it. so, for the first time, what's my name?"

"My dear Mr Devil, don't be offended if I happen to misname ee in my ignorance. Now aren't ee my lord Beelzebub?" asked Duffy.
"No! be damned. How could you confuse me with that upstart Beelzebub. He has never been heard of in the place where I live. I hear my horse shaking his bridle so, for the second time, I ask you my name."
"Pray excuse me" pleaded Duffy "and don't be vexed. I see you are a grand gentleman, no other, perhaps, than Prince Lucifer?"
"Lucifer, you make me mad to think that I could be taken for one of that mean tribe. But one such as you, born and bred in Buryan Church Town, can have no notion of the antiquity and dignity of my family. If you hadn't been the loveliest of Buryan ladies I would never have consented to spin for ee. Now, for the third and last time I ask ee, what is my name? But give me your hand love and let us be off for you can never guess it."
"Don't ee be in such a hurry, old gentleman." said Duffy. "Buryan people mayn't be so ignorant as you think them. They live near enough to St Leven witches to know something of devils and their dealings. You are TARRAWAY! You won't deny it."
"I am too proud of my ancient name to disown it" said the devil proudly. "I'm fairly beaten and it is provoking to be outwitted by a young thing like you. But, true as I'm a gentleman, if you won't come with me now, the time may come when you will wish that you had."
Thick smoke wrapped itself around Tarraway and, as Duffy shrank back, he vanished with a blaze of lightning and a peal of thunder which shook the house from end to end. This time there was a much stronger stench of brimstone left behind.

Duffy ran downstairs and, as she entered the hall, Joan tore in from the kitchen where the chimney top had fallen into the hearth. Pots and pans had been sent flying. The two women feared that the house was on fire for the whole place was filled with the smell of brimstone and scorching wool. Joan announced that she had a fit coming on and looked round for a comfortable place to have it. She had just found one when the squire rushed in dressed only in his hat, shirt and shoes.
"How are ee dressed so?" asked Duffy. "Where are your clothes?"
"I'd just got as far as Gramblers Grove" declared her husband "and couldn't find sight nor sign of last night's revels. Not so much as a patch of scorched earth. All at once I was blinded by such a flash of lightning and deafened by such a

clap of thunder as I never heard before. When I recovered me wits I was standing as you see me now, with all the clothes burnt off me. It's a wonder that I wasn't burnt alive and it must have been witchcraft, for there isn't a singe mark on me. Fetch me a coat, stockings and breeches woman, quick before anyone finds me in this state."

Duffy called Joan, freshly recovered from her fit, to accompany her upstairs. There they found nothing but ashes in the place of Tarraway's handiwork. All that was left was the squire's old, patched, darned and moth eaten clothes he had worn that first day outside An Jenny Chygwin's cottage when he had carried off Duffy to spin and knit for him.
"I aren't having they old rags" shouted the squire, in a rage. "Bring me proper clothes like I'm used to wearing, wife."
"These are all that's left" explained Duffy. "All your new clothes have been burnt up and destroyed. It must be the devil payin' ye back for disturbing his dance" cried Duffy and Joan added;
"Dosen't ee worry Maister, Duffy will soon have ee lookin' spruce again, wain't ee madam?"
"Up over stairs with ee" roared the squire. "Spin and knit for all you're worth for I shain't leave this house again until I have clothes fit to wear and be seen in."

Squire Lovell kept his wife at her turn for days on end but, try as she would, Duffy could spin no better than before Tarraway first arrived. All of her practice with the stocking at the mill was to no avail so, if she did manage to spin yarn, then she would still be unable to knit. A pellor was summoned and agreed with Duffy that the devil had paid the squire out for his interference. The wise man nailed a horse shoe to each door in the house and agreed to take the whole household under his protection.

Madam Lovell had rid herself of Cap'n Tarraway but now she couldn't get her husband out of doors and he was becomming more bad tempered by the day. The squire had forbidden Betty the house and it was some time before Duffy could slip away to the mill and ask the old witch to fetch a pair of the best stocking she could find in Penzance. Her husband wore them to go hunting. When he returned he was furious because the stockings were in rags from the furze and brambles and his legs were wet through.

"Art asleep, thou lazy slut?" called Squire Lovell up the stairs. "I can hear neither cards banging nor the turn spinning. If I don't get better stockings and new breeches I shall know the reason why. What the devil did I marry ee for, you lazy baggage?"

Duffy kept the loft door barred and threatened to 'card his face' if he entered. Master and mistress led a cat and dog's life for weeks. Those weeks felt like years to Duffy, shut up in the wool loft with not a soul to comfort her. She felt it would have been better for her to have gone with Tarraway and she wished and prayed that he might return but the devil was never more seen at Trove.

One Sunday, just before Christmas, the squire decided to scorn the sniggers of the townspeople and ride to church to hear the gossip which he had missed these past months. Duffy feined illness and, as soon as he had left on his horse, she fled to the mill. There she begged Betty to help her for, otherwise, she threatened, she would throw herself into the mill race and be done with life.
"Dosen't ee do such a thing my young beauty" said Betty. And, after twirling her thumbs for a moment or two she added "Leave us try a trick I've thought of. A woman should never despair of fooling an old man. And if that don't work then the old witch in me will see what she can do. Nobody never got out of a ditch by grunting. You spent too much time bemoaning your griefs rather than thinking how to get rid of 'em. Be off to church when the squire do ask ee next Sunday, which is Christmas day. And on the way back, when you de see me, wish me a 'Merry Christmas and a Happy New Year, when ee do come'. I shall wish ee the same. Then you must invite me, before the squire can stop ee, to come up and taste your Christmas beer. Don't ee be surprised at anything you see or hear or, if you are, dosen't ee show it. Now off home for yer life, before the squire de return and come lookin' for ee."
"Oh Betty" wailed Duffy, "I do hope you can help me for I can stand this miserable existence no more."
"There now my lovely" said Betty. "It id'n no fault of yours that you can neither knit nor spin for you never had a mammy to teach ee, only that old suss, Jenny Chygwin for a step mother. You never in your life shown me no scornful pride when you was Duffy Chygwin nor lately, since you been a grand lady. If you had I wouldn't have gone chasing for ee like I did that night. And no one can blame ee for deceiving Squire Lovell like you did. Lying and deceit come naturally to us poor women. Hasten home and leave the rest to me and hope for better times."

Duffy got home just in time to put the dinner on the table against the squire's return from church. The service had done the old man good and he was in a better temper than when he had left.
"Duffy, my dear" he said, "I wish you had gone to church, for all wanted to know where we have been these past weeks. Come along next week for the Christmas Day service. Today the women, curse their curiosity, were all for folding down my boot tops to see my fine stockings. They won't be so forthing if you are there next week."

On Christmas morning, Duffy, dressed as fine as any lady in Buryan, sat on the pillion behind her husband and they set off for church. After the service, a crowd gathered around the cross in the townsplace to sing carols and exchange Christmas greetings. Amongst the Cardews, Noys, Penders, Vivians, Gwennaps and other Buryan gentry stood Betty Chymellan in her steeple crowned hat and red cloak.

Duffy hailed her. “Good morrow to ee, Dame Chymellan, how are ee? I wish ee a Merry Christmas and a Happy New Year when ee do come. I hope you liked the sermon, and wasn’t the singin’ brave?”

“Thanks your honour” said Betty dropping a deep curtsey, and then she turned to all the other gentlefolk, addressing each by their name and curtsying to each, wished their honours the complements of the tide.

As soon as she had the attention of the crowd, at each curtsey, Betty broke wind and all the ladies looked round in some confusion. The Squire, believing them to be blaming him for the offence, became vexed and rode off with Duffy. Betty mounted the heaving stock, settled herself on her mount, jogged off with Dame Pendar and followed Squire Lovell down the road to Trove. As Betty caught up with the pair, Duffy called out to her.

“Now, Betty, be sure and come up and try our Christmas cake and ale.” The squire was too embarrassed by the incident outside the church to make any objection and so the invitation stood.

“I shouldn’t have minded any other day”, said the squire to Duffy later, “but all the Gentry will be here this evening and I want her on her best behaviour. Still,” he said, remembering the trouble he had been having since seeing Betty at the Devil’s Dance in the fugoo “one don’t like to offend the spiteful old witch for fear of her tricks.”

When the crowd had assembled in Trove Hall, Betty and Joan entered from the kitchen, holding foaming horns of liquor aloft. Squire Lovell, fearing another unseemly display should Betty again wish ‘good health to all of their honours’,

rose and shooed her back into the kitchen.
"You made me ashamed of ee today in the town place" he told her. "I don't want ee to do it again here at Trove. How could ee pay such little respect to the company?"
"Oh dear! Maister. You mustn't mind such a trifle as that for it will soon be the same with Madam there, your honour's wife if you keep her at the spinning. She won't be able to help it. 'Twas the same with me when I was a young woman, spinnin' all night and day. But one day the twaddling string broke, as they will with too much use, and over I went on my back and ever since I've been in this predicament. Now, don't ee think it would be a shame for your dear wife, Madam Lovell, if the same should happen to her and she become more of a embarrassment to ee than the ornament she is today, the dear of 'er?"
"I'm glad you told me An Betty and I'm some sorry to hear of your affliction. Now drink another flagon of beer. I shouldn't for the world that my darling Duffy should be in the same plight. Never more shall she spin from this very night. I would go bare legged for the rest of my life rather than such a mishap should befall my dear wife."

An Jenny's Picture

Frank Tonkin pulled up at the lonely cottage and got down from the cart. "Don't ee bother with the feed bag for the horse, Jan" said Frank to his apprentice. "He'll be alright there 'til we de find out what An Jenny de want we to do. Commost on in, booy". Jan looked a little nervous at the prospect of entering the cottage. "She wain't hurt ee" said Frank, with a laugh.
"I aren't so sure, Mr Tonkin" said the lad. "My faither told me some stories about she when I told un where we was workin' to today. Made my hair stand on end, some of 'em did".
"Don't ee take no notice a'tall me son. I've knowed An Jenny for as long as I can remember and we de get on 'ansome if you don't take no notice of her little funny ways. Your faither is just teasin' of ee. Commost on, we'd' best get in 'cos it don't do to keep she waiting".
The two men walked up to the cottage door, knocked and waited. They were soon let in by Aunt Jenny Tregurney, commonly known as 'An Jen' by the small community in which she lived. The men received a gruff "mornin' to ee" from the old lady and then had to wait in silence as she completed the task they had interrupted. The cottage could not be described as neat but neither was it dirty nor untidy. There was some order to the piles of clutter which occupied most of the space and only a few of the piles had top-knots of dust. Every beam had its bunches of hanging herbs, mostly still green. There were glass jars full of liquids in assorted colours, arranged on shelves. There was no upper floor to the cottage but, as was customary in those days, there was a talfat or platform at one end. This was where the old lady climbed up to sleep. Mr Tonkin broke the silence at last, much to the relief of Jan, who's unease was growing again in the strange surroundings.
"What do ee want us to do for ee, An Jen?" he asked.
"Scat down the talfat and take all the daub off the whole wall, planchon to hellin, and render un smooth and flat as the say of a still night" said An Jenny to the builder.
"Where are ee goin' to sleep to, An Jenny, if we de scat down your platform?" asked Mr Tonkin.

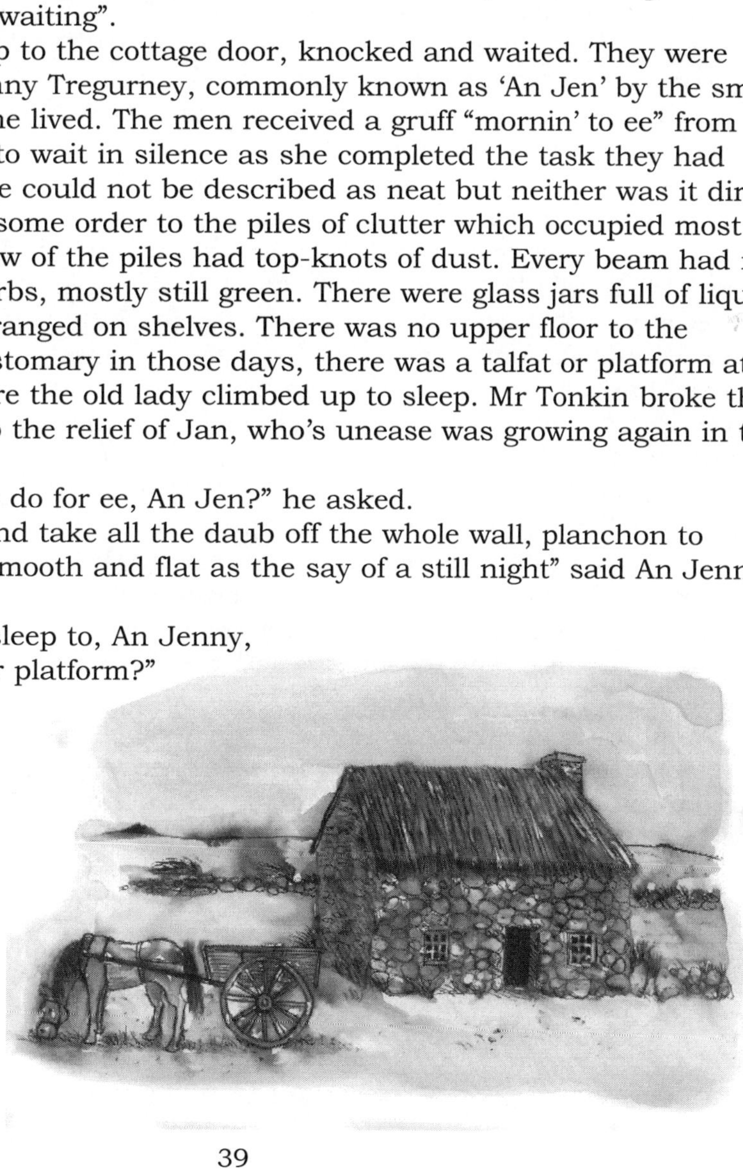

"Dosen't ee worry yerself about that my handsome, I shall find somewhere."
"But, what do ee want a plain, flat wall like that for anyhow?" asked Jan.
"I've a mind to have a pickcher painted on the wall" announced the old woman. "A grand pickcher, painted by Herbert Opie his self."
"He!" cried Mr Tonkin. "You wain't be able to afford te have he te paint yer wall, An Jenny. He de paint portraits for the gentry and he de charge a fortune for 'em as well. Take my advice. You have Herbert Trudgeon instead. He de paint off a good enough likeness and don't charge much more than the price of the ale he de drink while he's a paintin' of un neither. What ee want painted on yer wall any how?"
"What I de have painted is me own business for one thing and how much I de pay for un is the same. I shain't have no trashy Trudgeons in here. Herbert Opie is the man for me and I already paid un over the years. He've had the benefit of my powers and wisdom often enough and he de knaw just how much of he's success in the art trade he de owe to me. See that pickcher on the wall there." The old lady pointed to a small canvas in a dark corner of the cottage. "He've already painted that off for me. He knaw he got one more to paint 'fore I de die. I b'lieve I shain't keep ee all waiting long once tha's finished."
"We wouldn't want nothing to happen to ee, An Jen" said Jan. "We wain't want no portrait of ee to remind us of what you de look like cos, seem te me, you shall be here for we to look 'pon ee for a good many years yet, Lord willin'."
"None of us, not even me who de study such things, de knaw 'zackly how long we got, booy Janner, but I don't believe as how I got much longer to go. And anyhow, ee in't a portrait I'm havin' painted off."
"What are ee havin' on yer wall then An Jen?" asked Mr Tonkin.
"I aren't tellin' ee" she replied, "but you shall see when ee's done 'cause I got another job for the two of ee te do when the pickcher is finished."
"Have ee now An Jenny," said Jan "and what's that?"
"Thees 'll have te wait and see" announced the old lady as she disappeared through the doorway and stamped off down the lane with her herb basket over her arm.
"Don't do to make An Jenny teasy" said Mr Tonkin to Jan. "The folk round here de think a brear lot of she. Most cain't afford no doctors so she de make all the physic when anybody de fall sick. Good stuff ee is too, so they de say. And physic id'n all that she de make from her herbs, accordin' to some round 'ere. So, we'd be best off keeping she as sweet as we can. Leave us get started and do a good job for the ol' dear. That wall is about as straight as a dog's hind leg and we shall have to give un a good few coats to get un flat. Time to pitch to, booy."

The two men made a space on the floor of the cottage for An Jenny's bed and tore down the platform on which it had rested. They stripped off the mud daub that kept the wind from roaring through the cracks between the stones and pointed up the gaps with lime mortar. When An Jenny returned that evening she could see that they had done as she had asked and that the wall would soon be flat-plain from floor to apex. In the dry summer weather, a coat of plaster could be applied to the irregularities every day. By the end of the week the surface was flat and the final fine coat, the one which would receive the paint from Mr Opie, had been applied.

An Jenny seemed well pleased with the work. The agreed price was paid and the men were sent off to other work which awaited their attention. Before they were dismissed, An Jen reminded Mr Tonkin about the small task which still remained to be done.
"Ee shain't take ee long but I shall wan't un done as soon as the paint's dry mind" said An Jenny.
"Doesn't ee worry, my handsome," replied the mason "if ee' s only a small job, you leave we knaw a day or so before hand and we shall fit un in, round our other work."
A week or so later, An Jenny visited Frank Tonkin and asked him to come and finish the work as soon as he was able.
"I shall be up with the boy come Wednesday" announced the mason. "What ee want we to do, my handsome?
"I want a hole scat in the wall" said An Jen, "Shouldn't take ee long."
"Scat a hole in the wall! The one you had plastered and painted?"
"Ess, tha's right."
"But we shall end up outside if we do that." complained Mr Tonkin.
"You leave me to worry about that" said An Jen. "See ee Wednesday."

The two arrived early on the appointed day and were amazed when An Jen proudly showed them their plasterwork. The wall had been painted to represent . . . a wall. Not a simple cottage wall but one which might be seen in a grand mansion. It had cornices and carvings and niches filled with impressive statuary. The painted stones appeared to be cut smooth, square and regular and some were carved with classical motifs. It looked so real that when you glanced away from the painting, you were surprised to find yourself still in the tiny cottage.

Mr Tonkin looked puzzled as he stared at the painting but, after a minute or so, his expression changed suddenly. He turned and walked over to the small canvas which Mr Opie had painted for An Jen and then he looked back at the newly decorated wall. An Jen laughed as she watched him.
"Ess my son, they're the same. 'Zackly the same" she said and laughed again at his surprise. Mr Tonkin managed to overcome his confusion and bring his mind back to the job in hand.
"Where do ee want the hole put to, An Jen?" asked Mr Tonkin.
"There!" the old lady replied, pointing at a doorway in the painting, right in the middle of the beautifully flat end wall of the cottage. "That's where I want the hole and that's where you're going to put un, Frank Tonkin. That's what we agreed" said An Jen. "And I don't want no damage to the rest of the picture neither. The hole have got to be 'zactly where the door is drawed and nowhere else."
"We shall have to get a bit of oak for a lintel or the whole bleady thing'll come down and the rest of the cottage with un" said Mr Tonkin. "We underneath too, if we aren't careful. Dosen't ee worry though, An Jen, we shall be careful with yer paintin'."
"You better be. I got to go out to Morvah but I shall be back before dark. You going to have the job jobbed by then are ee?"
"We shall if we don't go home for croust" said Mr Tonkin. "Cummost on Jan, booy. I shall want you to get a bit of oak, thick enough for a lintel and you'd better be back here with un before I finished cutting through to the stones."

The boy ran off with measurements for the timber and An Jen soon followed him, leaving Frank to start the work of cutting the plaster away. He was a careful worker and it took some time to remove the render and expose the stones beneath. Frank then started work, cutting two pockets in the stone work to house the oak beam which would support the wall above. Jan returned, just in time for the timber to be inserted and wedged in place while mortar set around it.

Expecting to return home for their midday meal, the two had brought no provisions with them. "Leave us have a bit of a drink, Jan booy" said Frank. "We shain't have time for nothin' else but my ouzle's as dry as dust and I waint be no good to nobody without a drop of somethin' to ease un. See if you can find where she do keep her tay, lad."

Frank started removing the stones below the new lintel while Jan filled the kettle with water from the bussa and set it on the slab to boil.
"Aven't ee footched out that caddy yet booy?" asked Mr Tonkin. "I'm parched with all this lime dust flyin' about."
"I don't b'lieve she got no tea, Mr Tonkin." cried Jan searching through the cluttered shelves. "Hang on, what's this at the back here?" Jan pulled down a small tin box and opened it up. "We're all right, Mr Tonkin. I found the tay caddy. Kettle's on the slab so waint be long till ee's brewed. My soul and body! There id'n much tay in 'ere."

Jan soon produced a steaming mug and handed it to Frank.
"Don't look much like tea to me, booy Jan. You sure that was the caddy?"
"Ee must be Mr Tonkin. Do uh taste alright? I spec' ees some herby tea what An Jen de make."
"Well, booy, ee don't taste too bad. Could be a bit stronger though. Put a few more leaves in the pot booy."
"There idn' no more Mr Tonkin, best give un a stir."
"Poor old soul" said Frank, "what's she goin' to do when she de come home from Morvah, dry as dust from the journey?"
"Oh! She'll be alright Mr Tonkin. All she got to do is gather a few more of her herbs and don't have to pay nothing like we got to for shop tea."
"I s'pose you're right booy. Now, soon as you finish, you get a drop more mortar mixed up so we can make good when the hole is finished."
The two set to work and stones were taken out of the wall below the supporting timber.
"'Ere Jan," said Mr Tonkin, puzzled. "Go round to the outside and see what's behind this wall cos I'm through, but there id'n no daylight showin' yet."
Jan returned after a short while and said "That seem to be the end wall to me Mr Tonkin. I paced un out, inside and out and where you're to, that should be the end of the cottage. There idn' nothin' else outside."
"Dosen't ee be so plum, booy Jan. Here, leave us tear down the rest of the stones and then we shall have a better idea of what's goin' on."

Soon the hole was open from lintel to floor, following the outline painted by Mr Opie. The two were surprised to find another wall behind the first and a narrow space between, just big enough for someone to squeeze into. "Shall I light ee a candle so you can see better, Mr Tonkin?"
"You better had Jan and you'd best go in yourself for a geek, cos ee's a bit narrow for me"
"My gar, Mr Tonkin! I aren't goin in there. Ees black as pitch, seem me"
"Dosen't ee be so daft as you are. You'll be able to see with the candle."
It took some persuading to get Jan to squeeze into the space with his candle but eventually, reluctantly, the boy began to work his way along the narrow passage.
"What can ee see, Janner?" asked Mr Tonkin
"Nothin' at all" came a shaky reply. "Can I come out now, Mr Tonkin? I don't like it in here, There idn' no room to breath hardly. My gar!" shouted Jan, "I b'lieve I'm stuck. I cain't move a'tall Mr Tonkin! My soul! I cain't breath. Get me out, get me out!"

The boy's struggling and shrieking became rapidly more violent as his fear started to overwhelm him. Frank tried his best to calm the lad and believed that he had done so when Jan's screaming suddenly stopped. Then Frank realised that he could no longer see the flickering flame and that the boy must have fainted and dropped his candle.

It was now Mr Tonkin's turn to panic and at first he tried to squeeze into the narrow passage himself. When he realised that he was much too stout to enter, he pushed his arm into the space and was relieved to find that he could reach the boy quite easily. Reaching Jan was one thing but dragging him back out into the cottage interior took Frank a long time. The lad had crumpled as he had fallen and jammed into the space. Frank considered widening the hole to make the job of extracting Jan easier but he soon decided against this plan. He was a little afraid of the old lady's anger at spoiling the painting but much more frightened that the wall might collapse onto the boy if he were to remove more stones without further timber support.

It was exhausting work, turning the boy's dead weight in the small space so that his shoulders no longer bound on the rough masonry and Frank was almost fainting himself when he eventually dragged Jan out of the wall. When he had recovered a little from his exertions, Frank started to pull Jan towards the light and fresher air at the door end of the cottage. Jan lay still for a while and then, suddenly, his eyes burst open and he stared wildly at Frank.
"What's the matter with ee, my dear booy? What have give ee such a fright Jan?"
"There was somebody in there, Mr Tonkin; in the big room at the end of the passage. I thought 'he must be dead, walled up like that' but then he turned and looked right at me and he seemed to say something, not out loud but right inside my head. Frightened me to death he did Mr Tonkin."
"What did ee say to ee Jan booy?"
"I shain't never forget it, Mr Tonkin" said Jan, sitting up slowly. "I can hear it in my head right now.

'Full fifty years I've lingered in this room.
Today, once more, my love and I should meet.
You come instead and carry with you doom.
Our conjured plans you trample and defeat.'

And then the floor started to tremble and shake and next thing I know, I'm lying here. My gar, I'm passing out again Mr Tonkin, I'm feeling some headlight".
"You aren't headlight Jan, unless I am too. The floor seem to be moving"
The light in the cottage dimmed suddenly as An Jenny appeared and stood in the doorway. She gasped in delight as she saw the completed portal and, ignoring the two men, turned to the shelf where Jan had found the caddy. She snatched it down, wrenched it open and her screech when she looked inside turned Jan's face to parchment once again.
"They're gone!" she cried, looking wildly from Frank to Jan and back again.
"What's gone?" asked Frank.
"Four leafed clovers" sobbed the old woman. "Fifty years I've been saving them for this day. Where they to? I shain't live long enough to collect that many again." She ran, sobbing, towards the doorway in the painted wall. She threw herself through as a final shudder came up from the ground. The lintel snapped like a matchstick and the gable wall of the cottage shuddered and fell with a roar, crushing An Jenny beneath it.

Frank and Jan, at the far end of the cottage, escaped unharmed. They rushed to dig the old lady out from under the stones but there was no saving her. She was already dead when they reached her. They searched the wreckage in vain for another body. There was nothing but the rubble from which you might build a cottage wall, many pieces bearing traces of painted plaster.

In the days which followed the tragedy, Frank feared that his reputation as a builder would be ruined. He believed that his neighbours would blame the old lady's death on his poor handiwork but he need not have worried. The earthquake had been felt from Lands End to St Ives and several other properties had collapsed. No one came forward to claim the remains of the old lady's cottage which slowly crumbled back into the ground from which it had been built. Jan eventually became a partner in what developed into a very successful business. He built himself a house, married and raised a large family. Over his fireplace hung Opie's painting of the fateful wall which was the only thing of worth to survive the tragedy.

Frank and Jan? they enjoyed good fortune for the rest of their long lives. And no wonder! Hadn't they drunk tea made from four leaved clover?

Betty Stoggs and Jan the Mounster

Now Betty Stoggs was only her nickname but then, it was the only name she was ever called by. She was called Stoggs because she was so untidy about the legs and feet, and there was always holes in the heels of her stockings. She was no good at darning them and the lazy slut would never think to knit new ones. Betty was reared at Towednack, near Wheal Reeth, that's the bal where her faither was a miner. Praps Betty's failings were down to her Ma, a wretched, dirty woman who was a bit too fond of the drink.

I don't suppose it was Jan the Mounster that they had in mind when Betty's Ma and Da schemed and planned to get Betty a husband. Jan was a geat bear of a man and very uncouth in his habits. But it was Jan that Betty took a fancy to and before long it was found that Betty had 'met with a misfortune'. *Now* the old people were in a great hurry to marry the girl off and promised Jan money for Cheene and Clome (that's china and earthenware). Jan the Mouster was very greedy and he thought that he should have more than crockery for taking the girl on. Perhaps he remembered the state of his own stockings and Betty's failings in this area.

No time could be lost in making an honest woman of Betty so, off to Penzance went Betty's Ma to buy a four poster bed, an eight day clock in a mahogany case and a mass of beautiful clome and cheene on a new dresser. Jan was invited to the cottage to see the treasures and he hung his great turnip of a watch on the dresser to see how it looked. He must have liked what he saw because he told Betty's Ma that he would take the girl as long as he could have the bright copper warming pan which hung beside the dresser.

Soon after they were married, a baby's voice could be heard in the cottage of Betty and Jan the Mounster. Betty must have found the child a trial because she soon followed her Ma down the road to drink. The croshar woman, a great nasty 'suss' of a woman, became close with Jan's wife. The croshar woman pretended to sell crochet work from a basket but, under the collars and cuffs 'for the ladies to wear on Sundays and holidays', was a bottle of gin.

Jan soon became discontent with married life. Betty didn't bake bread because her mother had never shown her how to. Jan *demanded* bread and even left his watch behind one day so that Betty could judge the baking properly. Betty made the dough and no sooner had she put it to rise when who should arrive but the croshar woman. Betty had a noggin and then another. Next she had her fortune told. The kettle was boiled and a bit of fat pork was scrawled up on the slab and the dough was left to go sour and heavy.

When the crochar woman left at last, Betty raced to get the bread baked for Jan's homecoming but the child had been neglected all day and became troublesome. Desparate to start baking, Betty gave the baby the watch and opened it up so that he could see the pretty wheels running round. No sooner had she turned her back than the watch was dropped into the ashes and it stopped.

Betty washed the watch in some dishwater to get the ashes out of the works and wiped it with a bit of cloth, removing the ash but introducing pilchard bones and lint in its place. The bread had to be baked by guess and come out of the slab 'black as yer 'at and hard as adamant'. Jan couldn't even mark it but he said that his axe had struck a spark off the loaf. The watch was blamed and Betty swore that it had stopped by itself and that was the cause of the overbaking.

The next day, Friday, Jan went to the bal hungry and, after work, because it was pay day, he went to St Ives to have the watch set to rights. The watch maker soon found the ash, rust, bones and lint. On his return home, Jan nearly murdered Betty.

Soon both Jan and Betty were boozing regularly. The baby was further neglected and was often left alone while Betty went out gossiping. And then, when Jan came home one day, the door was open and the baby had gone. Betty told Jan that the door was locked when she left but of course, he didn't believe her. He remembered her lying to him to get out of trouble over the watch.

Neighbours were summoned and a search started which went on until dark. No trace of the child was found. The searching began again at day break and as the neighbours were gathering, the cat ran into the cottage, tail sticking straight up like a flag pole, and 'screeching fit to bust'. It ran round and round, in and out of the cottage, still screetching until one of the neighbours followed it to a furze bush and was overjoyed to see the baby sleeping on a soft spot of mossy grass 'as sweet as a little nut,' wrapped up carefully in some old drapes, and with all his clothes placed near, clean and dry. When they unwrapped the child, they found he was covered over with bright flowers, as we might put them round a babe in a coffin. The ferns had been pulled up high all around, so that no cold wind could reach the infant.

Everyone declared that the child never looked so handsome before. It was plain enough, said an old women, that the Small People had taken the child to wash it from top to toe and make it fit to be carried off. The filthy state of the babe must have made their task of cleaning him a long one for the sun had risen before they could finish. The child was hidden away, ready to be taken away the next night. The piskeys were never known to come for the babe, but everyone said that this affair worked a great change in Betty Stoggs and Jan the Mounster. The cottage and the child were kept clean and tidy. The boy's father and mother drank less, and lived happier for ever afterwards.

The Old Woman's Shift

My Gar!" said the old woman, lying in her bed, in her cottage, on the moors, near the Knill monument, high above St Ives. "What's that?"
Did she say the "My Gar!" out loud or just inside her head? It was difficult to say these days. It was very lonely in her tiny, tumbledown cottage and she often talked out loud to herself, just for the company.
Never the less, "My Gar!"

There was no light, or at least there shouldn't have been. But wasn't that just a little glow or a tiny gleam, over by the fireplace? There shouldn't have been a sound on such a still, moonless night as tonight but wasn't that a chink or a chunk? It wasn't mice. The mice only scuttled and occasionally squeaked. They neither clunked nor clinked, gleamed nor glowed, but something had!

The old woman lay absolutely still in her bed and listened hard. She plucked up the courage to open her eyes again and yes, there was the glimmer, very small but definitely visible. "My Gar, the cottage is afire!" she thought and froze even stiller (if that was possible). She tried a silent sniff. There was no smell of smoke, thank the Lord. But whatever could it be, this clinking, clunking, gleaming glimmer? Then, the voices started.

Were they outside or inside her head? The thumping was definitely inside her chest, she knew that but, yes, the voices certainly seemed to be outside, over by the fire place with the gleam and the clinks. And what voices! She had never heard such speech before. It was silvery and tinkling and only just perceptible. There were words but none she had ever heard in Christian company. What she did recognise was that the voices were angry. Well, maybe not exactly angry, perhaps quarrelsome. That was it. The speakers were arguing and, every time during the argument, when a point was decided, there would be a chink or a chunk, a clink or a clunk - of metal.

The tinkling talk continued for some time while the old woman lay stiff and still in her bed, not daring to make a sound, worried that the thump of her heart would betray her to her uninvited visitors. All night long she kept her eyes squeezed shut. Try as she might, she could think of nothing else to do except to repeat once more, inside her head, "My Gar!"

She woke in the morning as soon as the first gull began to screech. At first she dared to do no more than ease open her eyes a fraction, just enough to peer round the little house and reassure herself that she was alone. There were no sounds save those that ought to have been heard on a morning. There were no voices save for that damned gull. (Why did he have to make such a din every day?) She crept out of bed and examined her cottage from top to bottom. This took only a moment or two for there was only the one room and a few sticks of furniture. Nothing had changed since she had retired to bed the night before. It must have been a dream all the time. "Dreams! drive ee wild, don't they? Make ee mazed! A daft dream and nothin' else" she thought to herself.

She relaxed a little and began making preparations for the day. She lit a fire in the little stove and put the kettle on to boil. She cleared the table, putting the silver sixpence which she found there on the mantle shelf for safe keeping. "Hold hard!" she cried. "There hasn't been a penny piece in the house since last Toosday. There definitely waddn' no sixpence on the table when I went to bed last night" She sat down on her rickety chair and began to ponder until the kettle boiled. Then she made a drop of tea and put on a pot of porridge for breakfast and began working at all the jobs which had to be done to keep body and soul together in this cold, wet weather, out here on the moors and all with next to no money coming into the house.

The sun set early at that time of year. With no candles and precious little wood left for the fire, the best place for the old woman was in her bed until the gull called her at dawn. She dreamed all night of chinks and chunks, clinks and clunks, of silvery, tinkling arguments until she woke to find a silver threepenny bit on the table. And there was something else. She had carefully swept the floor before retiring to bed but here were mud and dry leaves by the fire side where none should have been.

She was disappointed. The mud wasn't much of a problem but only three pence today! Still that was ninepence in two days, more money than she normally had most *weeks*. That night she retired early again but she decided not to draw her curtain across the window. There would be a bit of moon tonight and the sky had cleared. There might be a little light in the cottage. Maybe tonight she would see her visitors more clearly.

The Old Woman's Shift

She tried hard to keep awake and to watch all night but life was hard and tiring for a lonely old woman and she was soon dozing. The latch on the door lifted so slowly that it made no noise at all. The door opened only a few inches but this was enough to allow a band of visitors to enter, carrying bulging sacks slung over their shoulders. Now, the hinges of the door had not been oiled since the old woman's husband had died and, careful though the visitors were, pushing at the door, there was still a creak loud enough to wake the old woman with a start (which she hoped would not be noticed).

There was a glow again and this time she could see that it came from a tiny lantern, on the floor, near the fireplace. There was the same silvery speech with the hint of bad temper. And there were the same clinks and clunks, chinks and chunks. This time the old woman could see that the sounds were made by the contents of the sacks. The visitors were taking plates, trays, all manner of coins, bracelets, rings, cups and other precious things from their sacks and debating who should have which item of treasure to take away as his own. 'Spriggans!' thought the old woman. Here was the very race of little people she had been told about by her Granny when she was a girl, here, in this very cottage. Until this minute she had imagined that spriggans were just pretend, made up by old people to entertain children and to keep them quiet for a while. Now, what had her Granny told her about spriggans, all those years ago?

Spriggans love treasure, gold, silver, precious stones and ornaments. They were honest fairy folk, not like some you could mention, and they found their treasures where they had been lost or where they had been hidden, long years before, and then forgotten about. They lived under the carns up here on the wild moors where they stored and guarded their treasures carefully. What were spriggans doing here, in the old woman's cottage? This place must be convenient for them to meet after their nightly searches and to divide up their finds amongst themselves before they dispersed, each to his own pile of stones under which he would bury his treasures.

"Look at what they got" thought the old lady to herself. "Me as poor as a church mouse and they, coming round here every night with treasure enough to keep me in luxury for the rest of me days." And a greedy, covetous thought came into her mind. The idea grew and festered as she watched the nightly share-outs. On each visit, when the arguments were over and the spoils divided up, the leader of the spriggans would get onto the shoulders of one of the others and place the smallest of the coins they had found that night on the table. Sometimes it was another six pence or even a shilling but often it was a

penny. Once, she woke in the morning to find only a farthing on the table.
"I haven't got nothin' but me little cottage, what might not last another winter with all these storms, me few sticks of furniture what's fallin' to bits and the few clothes I de stand up in" said the old woman to herself one day. "And they spriggans de come by my house every night carrying a king's ransom in their bags. Ee idn' fair a'tall. And all I de get is what they de care to leave behind. How am I goin' to keep meself goin' with nothin' to live on 'cept their leavings?" She conveniently forgot that she had managed to live very much more comfortably on these leavings since the visitations had begun. Envy had caught hold of her and stirred her dish of discontent until it began to boil over.

How could she get her fair share of the spriggans' booty? Her granny had warned her about the small people. "Spiteful they are, all of 'em" Granny had told her, "specially if they de catch ee spying on 'em or interfering with their ways." Each night the old woman seethed with anger. These spriggans were taking liberties, commandeering her home without a 'by your leave' and leaving their insulting tips behind. She went over her granny's tales about small people again and again in her mind and then - she remembered.

"The surest defence against the spite of spriggans, piskeys, knockers, the whole lot of them is to 'turn' a garment" was Granny's advice. Turning an item of clothing inside out while dealing with small people made them utterly powerless against you. That night the old woman peeped out of her bed at the spriggans before her fire and saw a heap of booty, bigger than any they had brought to her home for a week. It gleamed in the faint spark of light from their little lantern. It chinked satisfyingly as they sorted gold from silver, glass from jewels and fired up the old woman's discontent with her lot.

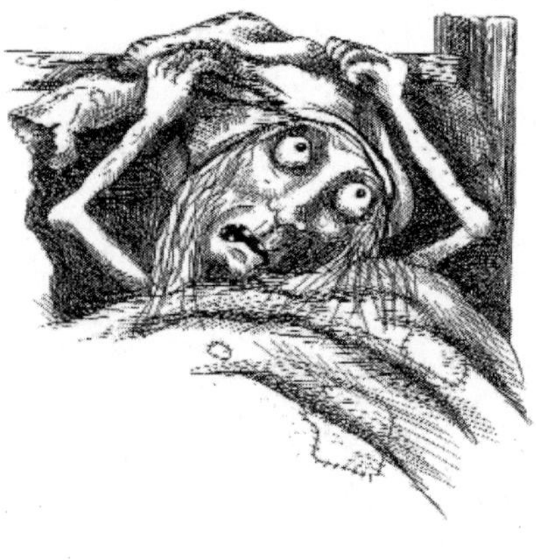

"I shall turn me clothes and then I shall drive 'em away and keep the treasure for meself" she thought. "But what can I turn? I only got me night shift on. How can I turn that without leavin' 'em knaw that I'm awake?"
She began to squirm and twist and turn in her bed. "I must go slow as a snail" she thought "or they shall see me sure as sure and then they'll scoot and take all their treasure with 'em. And I s'pec they shall find somewheres else to divi up their gold and I shain't even get me little bits of money they de leave behind 'em every night."

Slowly, stealthily, she struggled out of her shift. Her rheumatics made the unaccustomed movements agony but she dared not cry out. Eventually, one arm became free and then began to help its mate out of the second sleeve. Next, the whole shift was dragged slowly, oh so slowly and so stealthily, over the old woman's head. Once this manoeuvre had been completed she silently turned the garment inside out before struggling back into it once more.

The Old Woman's Shift

Almost an hour had passed since she had begun work on her plan. The treasures were now in neat piles and their owners would soon be bagging them up and carrying them away to the store rooms beneath the carns. It was 'now or never' thought the old woman. With a wild cry she leaped from the bed and spriggans scattered in panic before her. She gathered the heaps of treasure up in her blanket and lifted the lot onto her shoulder. The spriggans recovered their wits quickly and their leader advanced on the old woman, uttering words, dripping with menace and threat in his silvery tinkling speech. The old woman stood her ground and held the skirt of her shift in front of the spriggan's face to show him that the seams were now on the outside of the garment. His look of fury deepened and he reached out and touched the shift, cursing as he did so. The old woman began to fear that her Granny's trick would fail but she need not have worried because the spriggan king turned on his heel and led his whole band out of the cottage, leaving the old woman shaking but triumphant.

At first light, even before the gull had begun to screech, the old woman was up and away with a clanking bundle on her back. She walked down from the moors and into St Ives where she sold her treasures and deposited a great deal of cash in Steven's bank before visiting the land agent. There she purchased a neat, snug little cottage near the harbour and put her own little moorland cottage up for sale. Her next visit was to the carpenter's shop where she ordered new furniture for her new house. The old woman moved about the town, ordering and buying whatever she needed to live out the rest of her life in comfort and ease. The only problem which she had to endure after her adventure was that she could no longer bear the touch of her old night shift on her body, after the spriggan leader had cursed it. But then, she could afford as many shifts as she liked now. And she never breathed a word to a soul about how this had all come about for as long as she lived.

Now you might think that the old woman didn't deserve her comfort and ease. Hadn't she stolen from the small people? But then, you might say, hadn't the small people taken what wasn't theirs as well? One thing is clear. No one in Saint Ives ever learned how she had gained her wealth. But if that was so, how did we get to know about her? There's wonderful things in this world which we can't understand at all, sure 'nuff.

The Bahenna Brothers

The Bahenna farm, in the wild country between Nancledra and Zennor, was once a brave place. Jacob Bahenna had inherited it from his father, Aaron, but he didn't inherit Aaron's drive and spirit. The place had been allowed to decline. A bucket to catch the drips was Jacob's cure for a leaking roof. A broken window remained broken. A sick beast died for want of attention. Instead of keeping his farm, Jacob allowed the farm to keep him.

Jacob married Mary Trenance, the hard working, downtrodden daughter of a Towednack farmer. The marriage was not a love match. Mary saw in marriage, a means of escape from her father's tyranny while Jacob intended that his new wife would continue to work hard and to remain oppressed.

Mary Bahenna had two sons. The first born, young Paul, was Jacob's son in every respect and he was indulged and spoilt by his father. Ortho, the younger brother, inherited energy from his grandfather, old Aaron, and patient endurance from his mother. He worked hard, and any success that the farm enjoyed during Old Jacob's stewardship was entirely due to the younger son's efforts. Nevertheless, Ortho was despised by his father and his brother alike and after the death of Mary, Ortho took on his mother's role as household skivvy.

One mid-winter it was Old Jacob's turn to die. In spite of Ortho's hard work over the years, there wasn't enough value left in the farm to share between the two boys. The favourite, Paul, got the lot and Ortho got the rest. Paul Bahenna, however, was magnanimous and allowed his brother to occupy a tumbledown cottage which had been built for farm hands in more prosperous times. In addition, Ortho was allowed the use of a derelict orchard and a patch of ground which had been neglected for years and which Paul did not believe to be worth cultivating. There was a bowjy on this patch which was shared by two starving beasts which Paul had forgotten about; a broken down ox and an old shaggy donkey.

Paul Bahenna was not all heart, however. He demanded rent for the enjoyment of these assets and Ortho had to think hard about the best way to raise the money. He walked his land to assess its potential. The orchard was choked with

long grass, bramble and furze but there was rotten fruit on the ground showing that the trees could still produce. The two beasts in the enclosure were starving because there was barely enough grazing to sustain one of them. They were starving but they were still alive. The boy felt that he might make the place pay but, meanwhile, he had nothing to live on.

A near neighbour, Jimmy Hicks, had a small but prosperous farm nearby. Jimmy was an old school friend to whom Ortho now turned for advice.

"You're right about the orchard" said Jimmy. "My faither always said the apples were the best this side of Hayle."
"But you can hardly get into the place for all the furze and bramble" said Ortho.
"You come and work for me, booy" said Jimmy. "I'll pay ee enough to live on until next autumn. Evenings, I'll give ee a hand to clear the orchard. Feed the grass to they poor beasts of yours and they'll soon be fit for work again. Then you can hire 'em out for a few weeks. The ol' ox'll be some useful with plowin' this time o' year. They'll be fed while they're away and by the time they de come back, your grazin' will have recovered to keep 'em going. Burn all the bramble and furze in yer stove and that'll keep ee warm. I'll show ee how to trim the trees. Bit late for pruning but never mind. Got to be done. And you can burn the cuttings when the furze and bramble's gone."

The plan worked. By the end of the summer Ortho was exhausted but content with his lot. The sun had shone and the bees had buzzed in the orchard at blossom time. There would bc an abundance of apples in the autumn. The beasts were in good condition in their trim enclosure. Their bowjy had a new thatched roof.

Jimmy Hicks had a press for his own fruit and the quality of the Hicks' cider was legendary. The two friends decided that their apples would be pressed and

brewed together. The reputation of Jimmy's brewing would ensure that all the cider would be sold quickly and at a better price than Ortho could expect as a novice.
Autumn approached. The harvest was gathered and the apples were pressed. Once the cider was resting in its barrels, Ortho and Jimmy could relax in the evenings and plan for the future. Jimmy had learned good husbandry from his father while Ortho had learned that Jacob's lazy approach to farming brought poor rewards. One evening Jimmy told Ortho about the tradition of thanking the orchard for her bounty by pouring out a mug of the new cider beneath the trees. "Tis an old custom" said Jimmy "so the Vicar might not like it. Best do un at night. Might not be nothin' to un but it waint do no harm will uh? And ee might do ee all the good in the world."

When it was time to return to his cottage, Ortho decided to honour the old tradition that very night and set out with a flagon of cider under his arm and a mug in his spare hand. When he came to the orchard, he sat amongst his trees listening for the church clock to strike. Ortho had imagined that midnight might be the most propitious time for his task. Ortho was soon nodding under the influence of the strong brew he had drunk earlier. The lad woke with a start at the first of the midnight chimes. He quickly remembered where he was and why. He prepared to pour his offering of cider onto the ground when he was surprised by a sharp crack, followed by a shout.

"What ee doin? Theese goin' to waste that cider on the ground are ee?"

Ortho turned to face the sound just as a child step out, seemingly from the gnarled trunk of the largest and crookedest tree in the orchard. The child was curiously dressed in such old fashioned clothes that Ortho took it for a ghostly apparition and was about to turn tail and run then the child spoke again.
"Tis a shame to waste such fine liquor as that on the ground, my 'ansome. Why don't us enjoy un ourselves?"
"This is my best cider" stammered Ortho. "I b'lieve tis too strong for one so young as you."
"Young as me!" laughed the

'child'. "If 'twas daytime you might see something of me age in me face. I'm as old as the hills I am, and wiser too. I been the guardian of this orchard since the time of your grandfer's grandfer who planted it. And I been shrinkin' in size these many years while the orchard have been neglected. You men say that we can do wondrous things and so we can but we de depend on you more than you might imagine. The less you de think on we, the smaller we de become. Giants we was once and now look at us. Since your grandfer buried he's box under the roots of this tree, just before he died, no one have done a hand's turn to tend these trees until you started work here in the spring of the year."
"Why would my grandfather bury his box?" asked Ortho.
"Because, my 'ansome," said the little man, "he knew full well that his son was a worthless fellow and that riches would be wasted on him. Aaron believed that the blood of the Bahennas would run strong again after a generation or so. His wealth could lie fallow until that day. So, come on young feller. Hand me that mug. Pour out and we shall be merry and perhaps I shall be a bit taller in the morning. An perhaps you shall be a bit richer too."
"My chances of riches are scant" said Ortho to the guardian "but certainly I shall share the cider with you, if you believe the trees wain't mind".
"They! Mind? Your trees wain't mind my 'andsome. They know it was you who let the light back in and cleared the choking rubbish away. They're like me they are. Don't pay em no mind and they wither and die. The more attention they get, the lustier they de become and the more they yield every autumn. And I prophesy, young Ortho Bahenna, that your fortune will flourish with the orchard. You mind what I said about your granfer's box. That's still there, waitin' for ee, so leave us drink to that, my son."
Ortho filled the little man's mug and prepared to drink directly from the flagon. The guardian raised his cider and said;

'Here's to the trees and the apples they bear.
Here's to good friends and the cider they share.
Here's to the fortune that's waiting for thee,
Under the root of the crookedest tree.'

He drained his mug and tossed the empty vessel high into the air for Ortho to catch. There was a click as of a latch closing and when Ortho looked again, he found himself alone once more. He sat for a while, trying to make sense of what had happened when, all at once, it was morning and a very cold and damp morning at that. Ortho Bahenna rose from his hard bed, shook the leaves and earth from his aching body and trudged off home to the cottage to find some tools. He had some digging to do!

___***___

A week or so later Ortho and Jimmy were visiting the North Inn to sell some of their cider to the landlord. On this evening it so happened that Paul Bahenna was already seated in the parlour. He had been drinking heavily as usual and

was listening to the stories told by a wandering droll teller so he didn't notice his brother coming in from the cold. The old man was telling the tale of the beasts in the barn receiving the gift of speech every Christmas Eve and how they told rare secrets to each other and, if a man were to hide and listen to them, then he might learn great wisdom. Nobody ever did because they were either in the church, getting the great wisdom of the Christmas story, or in the pub getting too drunk to know wisdom when they heard it. The greatest wisdom of all was to be had from the two beasts which were present at the birth of Christ, the Ox and the Ass.
Everyone in the inn enjoyed the old man's story but it made the greatest impression on Paul. He determined to test out the tale but was loath to give up his Christmas Eve revels in the pub. The next day he had worked out a way to enjoy both activities and he called on Ortho.
"Have ee still got they two old broken down beasts, Ortho Booy?" asked Paul.
"Ess I have" said Ortho.
"And do ee still keep em in the old bowjy?"
"Ess I do."
"Well then, I'll leave ee off a pound from the rent if you de call for me at the North Inn at half past eleven on Christmas Eve and make sure I de get to the old bowjy before midnight. Only a pound mind, I shall expect rest the of the rent on Christmas morning. I'm a bit short meself this quarter and the bank is pressing me to pay."
"Dosen't ee worry theeself, brother" said Ortho. I got to call at the bank in Penzance tomorrow. You shall have the rent come Christmas."

A few weeks later, on Christmas Eve, Ortho did as he was bid and, accompanied by Jimmy Hicks, fetched his drink be-fuddled brother from the inn and helped him to the bowjy just before midnight.
"Both the beasts in there are they?" Paul asked.
"Ess they are but whatever do ee want to know for? You never took no interest in em before" said Ortho.
"Private business me son, nothing you need worry yerself about. You two get yourselves off home now and make sure you come up to the farmhouse in the morning with the rent, Ortho booy. Ee's due Christmas morning. I hope you got un all or you'll be out on your ear, my son. You knaw that the bank is pressing me to pay."
"I got the rent" replied Ortho, "dosen't ee worry. And I haven't forgot that you let me off a pound for tonight neither".
"Ess, alright I s'pose" said Paul. "Now, get off home, the pair of ee."

The church clock had just struck the first note of the midnight chimes as Paul crept into the stable. There was a strange, subdued commotion going on inside and after a few seconds, Paul was astounded to hear speech coming from the stalls.

"Old place is going to rack and ruin" said the Ox.
"Been let go" said the Ass.
"There was a fortune here once" said the Ox.
"Dug out of the ground now" said the Ass.
"No future for he that own it" said the Ox.
"Best be sold up" said the Ass.
"Take what he can from it and leave" said the Ox.
"Bank'll make un sell anyhow" said the Ass.
"Who'll buy?" asked the Ox.
"Matter-do-uh?" the Ass replied.
"Be enough for un to go abroad?" asked the Ox.
"Enough to start again in the New World" said the Ass.

The midnight chimes complete, the two beasts lapsed back into silence. Paul Bahenna, pale as a ghost and much sobered by what he had heard, went home to a sleepless night. He accepted the rent from his brother in the morning and waited for the banker's clerk to call for the quarter day dues. He was only a little short of the required amount but was told by the clerk that the bank insisted that he should avoid further losses and sell up. There was already a buyer who had offered enough to clear the debts and leave Paul with sufficient cash to try another venture, perhaps in Canada. Paul accepted the offer and, before the week was out, he had packed up, left for Plymouth and booked his passage to a new life abroad.

On New Year's day, Ortho Bahenna had invited Jimmy Hicks to dinner and the two met, not in Ortho's old cottage but in the Bahenna Farmhouse. A jar of best cider was broached and the two friends toasted the Bahenna farm and the New Year.

"He's gone then?" asked Jimmy.

"Gone for good. Sailed this morning" said Ortho.

"Old place is gone to rack and ruin?" asked Jimmy.

"Been let go. But on the mend now" said Ortho.

"Was there a fortune?" asked Jimmy.

"I dug un up" said the Ortho.

"No future for he that owned it?" said Jimmy.

"Took what he could and left" said Ortho.

"Do he knaw who bought the place?" asked Jimmy.

"Matter-do-uh?" Ortho replied.

"Yours now" said Jimmy.

"And still gold left in Grandfer's box" said Ortho.

The two friends laughed, shook hands and settled down to dinner.

Tom and Giant Denbrass

Tom surveyed the field. His mother had sent him here to pull weeds but he had other ideas. 'Weeds aren't the problem here' he thought to himself, 'they git rocks need shifting if we're going to grow anything in this field this season'. Tom strode over to the nearest boulder, bent down and gave it a tentative tug. The rock stayed where it was. Tom stood up and contemplated the size of the task he had set himself. He removed his jerkin, spat on his hands and bent down to get a firmer grip on the monster rock. Tom's face reddened and beads of sweat appeared on his brow. The rock held fast. Tom was not one to give up and he increased his effort further. His colour deepened to purple. Tom's frame began to quiver. He was almost at the end of his endurance when there was a tearing sound and the rock shot skywards. Tom found himself on his back, on the ground, with the enormous rock pinning him down.

Tom soon recovered himself, eased the rock from his belly and stood up. He rolled the boulder to the edge of the field and returned to the gaping hole he had made.

"I'll soon fill that up when all of these other rocks are over there, with their cousin" he said and addressed himself to the next offending chunk of granite. He strained, grunted and quivered and soon a second rock joined the first at the field's margin. In five minutes a third had joined the pair and made the beginnings of a heap. By croust time the heap was a large pile and the field was pockmarked with huge holes, the vacant, erstwhile resting places of the pile's components. Around each gaping hole there was a pile of ginger or grey subsoil which had been dragged to the surface by Tom's efforts.

Tom was extremely pleased with himself but close to exhaustion by the time his mother arrived to see how the weeding was progressing. The Spring had been cold and wet. It was now summer and this was the first patch of dry weather for months. Planting must be done now. Any more delay would mean a disastrous harvest.
"Still," Tom's mother thought to herself as she walked along the lane, "boy Tom will have dug the weeds by now. I'll get he to level the plot tomorrow and we can think about planting next week if the weather de keep fine like this."
"How have ee got on, my son?" she asked from the other side of the hedge.
"I've done handsome, Mother" answered Tom proudly. "See what I done."
Tom's mother looked and her jaw dropped.
"My gar, you git heathen good for nothing" she exploded, "What have ee been doin' of all day? Here we are, nearly Midsummer and all behind like the cow's tail and you spent all day diggin' holes! You're s'posed to have this plot ready for plantin' in a day or two and look at un! Clay and rab spread all over what little good soil we got. Nothin' wain't grow in that you daft lummox. I ought to give ee a tight cobbin, damn ee all into heaps (make me say the words). You'd try the patience of a saint, boy."

What happened next was entirely strange to Tom. He had not experienced anything like it in any of his seventeen years. His mother sat sown on Tom's pile of stones, threw her towser over her head and started to shake. Strange moans came from under the towser. Tom's mother was crying for the first time since she was a child.
"Whas-a-marra-with-ee Mammy?" he asked after a moment or two.

Tom's mother emerged from beneath the rough towser to reveal a tear-stained face which alarmed Tom even further.
"My dear Mammy, you're lookin' whisht as a winnard! Are ee very bad?"
"Very bad!" his mother screamed. "You git guckoo! You're enough to make anybody very bad you are. You aren't nothin' but a boutigo, kieekin' when you ought to be lousterin'. And thees'll have to louster all your life for you haven't got brains enough to scheemy."

She had vented her spleen and had a good cry. Tom's mother could now try to feel a little better disposed towards her only son. Fond as his mother was of the boy, desperate measures were called for if they were to survive until next year.
"I shall have to think what's best to do, Tom boy" she announced. "You're a fine git boy and strong as an ox. Just look at that heap of rocks you shifted this morning. But shiftin' rocks wain't feed

us, Tom. I shall have to hire in some sensible help and hope we got enough time to raise a crop. But I cain't feed three on what's left in the store room. You shall have to go out into the world and find your own way me son. Find somebody who de want rocks tore out of the ground or find somewhere where a git daft bull of a boy can earn his bread. God bless ee, my 'ansome. It will break me old heart to see ee go but go you got to. There idn' nothin' else to do about it at all.

At dawn on the following day, Tom's sorrowing mother sent her only son out into the world to fend for himself.
"Dosen't ee worry about me Mammy" cried Tom. "Now then, I got to walk to Marazion and if I keep the Mount in front of me, I cain't miss the town, is that it?"
"That's right, boy. Now, who have ee got to ask for when you de get there?"
"Mr Honey Chygwins, Mammy" replied Tom.
"*Mayor* Honey Chygwins, boy" his mother corrected him. "Tell the mayor who you are and who yer faither was. We all used to be friendly years ago, Honey, Old Tom and me. You was only a little tacker when Honey last saw you but he'll remember me sure enough. Mayor Chygwins will give ee a job boy or else send ee to somebody who can. I'm sure you'll work hard. Do as you're told and you should be all right."

Mayor Chygwins was very pleased to see Tom and hear that he was in need of a job. There was a load of beer for St Ives standing in the yard and no one free to deliver it.
The Mayor could see immediately that Tom was a fine strapping fellow and he hired him on the spot. A team of oxen was yoked to the dray in the yard and an extra barrel was brought out for Tom to drink, and for him to treat anyone he should meet on the way. Tom, proud to be a working man rather than a burden to his mammy, set off for St Ives.

A mile or so beyond Crowlas, Tom came across some men who were struggling to load a tree onto a cart. The tree was destined to become one of the roof timbers of a new church they were building.
"Stand back, boys" cried Tom as he grabbed the trunk of the tree and heaved it up onto the bed of the cart. Soon the crown was pulled on board as well and Tom climbed back onto his dray to continue his journey.
"Where ee goin' my handsome?" asked the gang leader.
"To St Ives with this load of beer from Honey Chygwins" answered Tom.
"You wain't get through that way, boy" he was told. "Old Denbras have blocked up the road with one of his hedges. The old man is extending his estate I believe."
"What!" roared Tom, "blocking the King's Highway? I shall have something to say to he when I see un."

"You will, will ee?" said one of the builders. "Old Giant Denbras is twice the size of you my son, big as you are, and have seen off many who have tried to thwart he's aims"
"He can try" boasted Tom. "Nobody else have managed throw me in a fair fight or a foul one."

A little further along the highway Tom came across the reported hindrance. A mighty hedge had been thrown up and a gate had been let into it where it crossed the road. The gate was locked and barred. Tom, in his impetuous way, ran full tilt at the gate and smashed it away and then proceeded to drive his dray through the gap he had made. The track from the gate led to the courtyard of a mighty castle and, as the dray approached, out ran a yapping little dog, followed by the old giant himself, rubbing his eyes. The giant was huge, about twice Tom's size but he was old and big bellied. His teeth were worn to stumps from grinding the bones of the sheep and goats which he ate raw each day.
"Hallo! Who do you think you are, you scrub, to drive in here and disturb my nap? Hello! Is the beer for me? I didn't expect any."

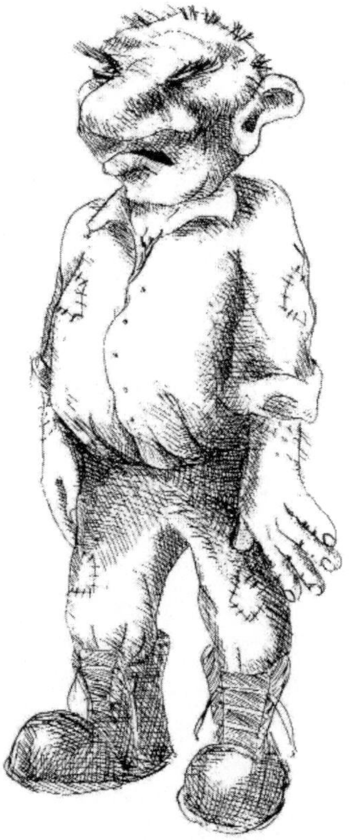

"You're welcome to a drink, my old beauty," said Tom "but I am on the way to St Ives, along the old road, and the right road too, in spite of you and your hedge."
"Thou art a saucy young whelp, spoiling my after dinner nap. Use the right-about way or I shall pick a twig and drive ee out."
"Don't crow too soon, my old cock" said Tom but the giant's blood was up. He strode down the valley and tore a young elm from the ground. Turning, he walked slowly back up hill, ripping branches from the tree, fashioning it into a club. Seeing what Denbras was about, Tom unloaded the huge barrels from the dray which he then turned over. Tom had plenty of time for this because Denbras was so slow puffing his way back up the hill. Tom pulled the wheels off the axle tree and then drew it from its mountings. He used one wheel as a shield and the axle tree as a buckler. He turned to face his opponent, still struggling up the hill.

"If you're for a fight then come on, old man" cried Tom. "I shall match my axle and wheel against your elm tree." But Tom saw how bleary eyed the old man had become and what poor condition he was in for the fight. He determined to tire the old fellow out and avoid wounding him even though he had many chances to do so. When Denbras slipped and fell after Tom had parried one of his clumsy blows, the lad helped him back on his feet and gave him a drink of beer.

Tom & Denbrass

The sun was nearly down when Tom sought to end the battle as swiftly as he could and gave the giant what was intended as a tickling blow below his ribs. Tom was poor at judging his own strength and the thrust pierced the giant's belly and came out near his backbone. Tom was much grieved to see the harm he had done to the old fellow.
"Cheer up. You'll do again. I'll do me best to mend your wound" said Tom. "Who would have thought your skin was so thin?"
Tom drew out the axle and the giant roared in pain as his blood ran out and down the hill like a mill stream.
"Stop your bellowing and hold your hands over the holes" said Tom "while I cut some turfs to stop them up." When he had dressed the wounds, Tom knocked the top out of a barrel and held the beer to the giant's lips that he might drink. "Drink up my hearty and we shall have some good play yet."
"It's no use, my son" groaned Denbras. "I feel I shall kick the bucket soon enough. No one can say but that I died in a fair fight. I like thee better for thy fair play than any other man I have ever fought. 'Fair play is good play' as they say. Thou art a true Cornish booy and I love thee like a brother. All my relations are dead so you shall be my heir. All my lands and treasures I give to ee. My breath is getting short so bow down to hear my dying wishes. The names of the dogs which guard the caves of my castle are Standby and Holdfast but tell no one else this. All my lands and the beasts on them I give ee, only bury me decent under a barrow and don't let any abuse me when I'm gone. Be kind to the dogs and my tame cattle, poor things, I am as sorry to leave them as if I were their faither.

Tom held the old giant's head in his arms and waited while he struggled for more breath. "Tom," said the giant "above all things I wish to be buried according to the fashion of the old people of this land. But first help me to the top of the hill where I used to delight to see the first glimpse of the rising sun or sit at eve, looking over this beautiful land to the sea, with my tame cattle sporting around me on the dewy heath. Help me take one last look at the hills where my race has so long lived."

Tom helped the old man to his favourite seat on a flat stone on the hill's summit. Similar stones lay all around him, ready to be drawn about the giant

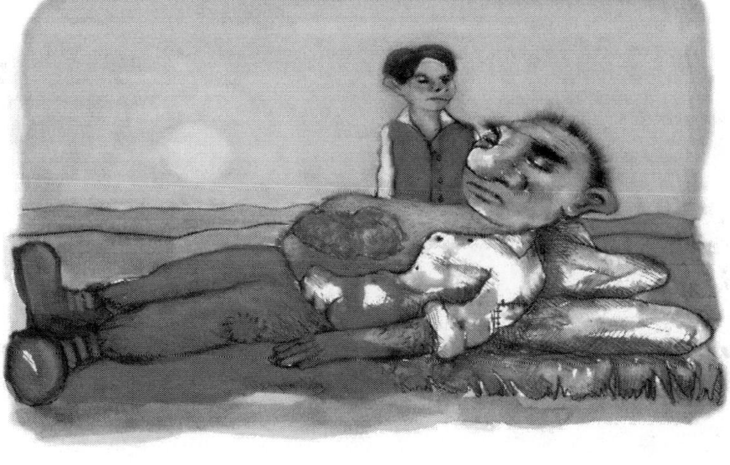

after his death. Nearby lay a huge quoit to cap the whole. Denbras looked his last over his realm. "My eyes can no longer see the glorious sun" he groaned "and now, farewell to thee, my dear. In thy arms I die content, my son."
"My dear daddy, don't go yet" said Tom. "Stop a moment or two more and tell me what shall I do about your wives. You haven't eaten them all I suppose, as they say you have in the towns and villages around."
"Oh the wretches!" cried Denbras. "The Devil fetch them for their slanderous tongues. I had hoped to die at peace with all the world. Now listen. Long before my first old woman was dead, the wretches flocked round here to see if I would take home another wife. I flung stones at 'em but still they came. The whisht lookin' ones were the worst. I'd tell 'em they weren't up to the rough wear and tear of hill-country life. They would take no denial and one by one, they died and I buried every one under the barrows all around us."
The anger caused by the mention of that slander made the turf plugs blow out of Denbras' wounds and he bled afresh. He turned to Tom and said "and now my son, I'm glad to leave this wicked world." He bowed his great head and died.

Tom put Denbras' hands on his knees and then pulled the flat stones upright about the giant's stiffening body. Then he hastened down to where he had left his oxen. He found them at ease and chewing their cud. He replaced the great axle and wheels of the dray, loaded up the beer and drove it through the giant's domain, out of the other gate and on to St Ives. The beer was delivered and Tom drove the empty dray back to Market Jew where he arrived on Midsummer's Eve to find the town and all the hills about, ablaze with bonfires. The brewer was pleased to see Tom back so soon and offered him a place as his dray man for a year.
"I could never wish for a better job than this" said Tom, "with beer flowing and good wages and grub. But my old daddy died yesterday and has left me his lands up in the hills and all his wealth. I must go tomorrow and take possession of my inheritance and finish burying the old boy decently.

On his way back to the hills of Towednack, where Denbras' castle lay, Tom called in to say goodbye to his mammy and tell her of his good fortune. He also called in on Joan of Crowlas whom he had been courting for a long time. He told her about his luck as well and asked her to come away with him and share in it. Joan gathered a few possessions and left home to throw in her lot with Tom.

When they reached Denbras' castle, Tom called the dogs by the names which the giant has told him to use and they allowed the pair into the castle caves without so much as a growl. There they found tin, gold and silver such as was usually found in giants' castles in days of old. Before he would allow himself to enjoy his new found wealth, Tom told Joan that he must keep his promise to the old giant and finish the burial he had started a few days earlier. The two climbed to the top of the hill where Denbras lay. Joan gathered green oak branches and flowers which she lay around him. Tom placed the giant's great sling and club beside the body and then they started work on the barrow. The pair worked all day, collecting the stones which lay all about and piling them round the uprights. At evening, when a decent pile had been made round the grave they used levers to move the great capstone up the sloping sides of the monument to lie on the upright stones which Tom had used to first enclose the body. This slab was too heavy for even Tom to move without mechanical assistance. The barrow they had made was as great as any other on the Towednack hills but this didn't stop the pair, from time to time, adding more stones to the cairn of the giant's resting place.

---***---

Tom and Joan settled into their lands and possessions and raised a large family. They kept to themselves in their wild fastness in the hills. No one in the area knew about the death of the giant and his memory kept visitors away. It came as something of a shock to Tom when, after a few years of peaceful, private living in his realm, there came a loud knocking on the castle door. Before Tom could answer the summons, there in the castle court stood a travelling tinkard with his hammer in his hand and a leather bag of other tools on his back. The tinkard had employed his hammer in smashing down the gate across the King's highway which Tom had repaired after the giant's death.

"Hullo my man. And where are you bound for?" cried Tom.

"I'm on my way to St Ives, along the King's Highway" answered the tinkard "and I want to see if the mistress of this place wants any pots or pans mended, in spite of all your hedges and gates. The people round here are complaining that the giant is hedging in all of the country. I've never seen a giant yet that I like and you, my great strapping boy, must be his eldest son. Bring the old fellow out. Or shall we try each other's mettle first? What say you? Shall it be quarter-staves or single-stick?"

"Staves or sticks, fists, slings or wrestling, I'll try my strength with any man in any play you like. Make your choice" said Tom.

"I'll match my blackthorn stick against any timber you can raise" replied his opponent.

Tom picked up an oaken bar which the tinkard had broken from the gate and shouted 'GUARE' to start the play. Immediately the tinkard spun his stick and passed it from hand to hand, flicking out blows at Tom so rapidly that he had no time to parry. Those few blows which Tom managed to deliver rained down with the force of a sledge hammer but made little impression through the tinkard's heavy leather coat. Tom's nose was streaming blood and one eye was shut before his oaken cudgel was struck from his hand. Jack the Tinkard was as far in advance of Tom in skill as Tom had been ahead of Denbrass. The tinkard, however, was courteous and allowed Tom time to recover his cudgel whenever it was struck from his hand.

Tom thought it likely that he had a devil to contend with but he could see no forked tail or cloven hoof about the tinkard and concluded he must be a man. The coat of bull hide which he wore was a wonder. It was seamless and hard as iron. Although it was covered with thick curly bull hair, it rang like a bell whenever Tom's cudgel struck it a blow.

"Thees'd better give in, booy" advised the tinkard. "I can see that thee dosen't knaw this play. I could have scat thee flying a dozen times if I had a mind to. Science is more valuable than brute strength in this game, my handsome."
The tinker put the thorn stick into Tom's hands and showed him a few of the simpler cuts and passes. The two men continued the play and Tom fared better with the few tricks the tinkard had showed him. As they fought, a friendship began to form between the two which was destined to become stronger the longer they spent in each other's company. Meanwhile, Joan had wondered what was keeping Tom from his midday meal. He was usually ready for it an hour or more before noon. She came out from the castle to look for him and was surprised and not a little gratified to see a stranger in the yard. For all she enjoyed her life with Tom in the hills she sometimes hungered for news of what was happening in the wider world.
Why didn' ee tell me we had a visitor, Tom?" she asked him. "All we got is beef and pease. Come on into the kitchen the pair of ee but first, Tom, wash off all that blood theese art grouted with."

The Tinkard took off his great bull hide coat and Tom saw that he had been beaten by a man of average size, with a cheerful face and a mop of dark curly hair. Joan made the stranger welcome by tapping a cask of the strongest beer, intended for the next feastentide. This was placed on the board along with barley bread, cream and honey. There was also a flask of mead to drink at the end of the repast. Tom promised the stranger that they would go hunting for game in the hills so that they might enjoy a better meal in the evening.

Tom had a brief, three hour nap after the meal and the Tinkard took the opportunity to see to all the pots and pans in the kitchen which needed mending. When Tom awoke he suggested that they put off their planned wrestling match until the next day to give them more time for the hunt. The dogs were called out. Tom picked up his sling which he used for hunting. The tinkard cut a young elm sapling and fashioned it into a bow staff. He found, in his never-failing leathern bag, a cord with which to string the weapon and the two set out. Along the way, the tinkard cut shafts from the thickets they passed and fashioned them into arrows. Tom was fascinated to see this work as he had

heard of bows and arrows but had never seen any.
The tinkard killed many more beasts than Tom managed with his sling and stones. In one hour, Tom's children who were following after the men, gathered up enough meat for a week. Joan was delighted to see such a store because she could now furnish meals fit for a guest for as long as the stranger stayed in the castle.

While Joan and Genevra, her oldest daughter, prepared the evening meal, Tom showed the Tinkard over the castle. The visitor noticed scratches on some of the stones forming the walls of the castle and, recognising these as symbols and not accidental scratches, soon found a secret store hole in the thickness of the castle walls. Inside the store were wonders of gold, silver, amber, crystal and pearl which made Tom gasp. The tinkard was more interested in other 'lumber', as Tom described it, which the giants of old had hidden in the cavity. There were tools which the tinkard recognised and iron bars which he was very pleased to have. Joan called the men to their evening meal and was as surprised when the tinkard hung a string of pearls around her neck as the children were when Tom scattered beads of crystal and amber on the floor for them to use as marbles.

The tinkard had eaten many a pie in his journeys through Cornwall from the Tamar to Towednack but none so fine as that which Joan set before him, made of fresh rabbit and hare with venison, seasoned and flavoured with herbs she had gathered that day. Rich cakes with honey, milk, cheese and cream from the dairy finished the meal. Joan was pleased to see her guest so content and the children happy playing with the amber and crystal beads. Genevra delighted to wear some of the trinkets which the tinker had found. When the meal was over, the stranger was shown his place to sleep which the women had strewn with flowers and soft rushes they had gathered while the men were at the hunt.

While the breakfast was being prepared the next morning, the tinkard told the family his story. He had been born in a county, far to the east where he had been raised on the moors by a gang of tin streaming men. He didn't know which, if any of the men was his father. The gang was visited regularly by merchants from a town close by who exchanged food and other necessities for the tin from the streams. One of the merchants, taking a fancy to the boy, gave him the name Jack and took him off to the town to learn tin dressing and many other skills. When he had come of age and had heard about the rich tin streams in the far west, he had journeyed thence to try his luck. During his stay in Marazion, he heard that a terrible old giant still lived in a stronghold in Towednack. He little thought that the 'terrible old giant' would turn out to be no one but his new friend Tom.

In the weeks that followed, Tom and Jack competed in all of the manly games known in those times. Where brute strength was needed, Tom won, but where science was required, Jack prevailed. In the famous wrestling match Tom put Jack the tinkard on his back time and time again but, mindful of the hurt he had done to Giant Denbras all those years ago, he placed him there as gently as if Jack were a babe. While they were thus occupied they didn't see the two intruders who had come across the broken gate which neither Tom nor Jack had thought to mend. These men from Tregendar had dared each other to enter the giant's domain and were spying on the wrestling going on in the castle yard. One noticed Joan and Genevre who were watching the sport while working at their distaffs.
"Isn't that Joan of Crowlass?" he whispered to his mate. "She and me were very friendly years ago but she left of a sudden, one midsummer night, and has never been heard of since. Do ee think she is the lady of Denbras' castle, the old giant's wife?"
"I b'lieve you're right and isn't that feller young Tom from Bowjeyheer, growed up? asked the second intruder. "And didn't he disappear at about the same time? Has the old giant died? No one has heard from him for years."

That night, word spread like wildfire and by morning, news about Joan being the lady of the giant's castle had reached St Ives, Mousehole, Market Jew, St Just and all places in between. Every woman with the slightest claim to kinship with Joan of Crowlass was converging on the Towednack stronghold. Tom and Jack had left early with the children to try out new bows which Jack had made for them all and Joan was left alone to deal with all the visitors. Early in the afternoon she glanced out of the look-out and was surprised to see a great company of women and children climbing the hill towards the castle.
"My dear cousin Joan, how glad I am

to see ee" the foremost called out in greeting with hands outstretched. "How is the sweet old dear, your husband? You are very comfortable here with the giant but I thought as how I should knit a nightcap for the dear's head against the cold winter nights up here on the hills. Where are all the children? Leave me see the dears."
"I can't say as how I ever clapped eyes on ee before this minute" said Joan.
"Dear me, I'm a pretty near relation too, for my husband's sister married a cousin to your uncle's wife. I never believed it when they said as how you had gone off into the country with great long Tom the hedger from Bowjeyheer. I always knew you had done better than that for yourself. Better be an old man's darling than a young man's slave."

Fortunately one of the dogs, sensing discord began to growl and this set off the others. This gave Joan a chance to form a scheme to rid herself of the intruders. "I might be glad to see ee another time" she told the women "but the old giant is sleeping now and can't abide being disturbed. He often sleeps for weeks at a time. I knaw his regular times of waking and always keep a few goats to hand for un, or else he would have devoured me long ago. If these here dogs de wake him then none of ee shall see the Digey again. Make haste home while your skin is whole. You had better wait 'till we de send for ee before coming again."

When the hunters returned, Jack went down to the gate and secured it against further intruders. The next day, Jack was for leaving to continue his quest for tin.
"If it's only tin that theese art searching for, we got plenty here in the castle. I don't care for such trash myself. All it's good for is to buy land and I got as much land as anyone could want. Have as much tin as you wish, only stay, Jack booy. You shall never want for beef nor honest homespun clothes. I love thee like a brother and Joan and the young ones feel the same.

Jack was as loath to leave as Tom was to let him and it was decided that he should make his home in the castle. He would wander the country whenever he had a fancy to but the castle gates would always be open to him. The tinkard had many things to teach Tom and Joan. He made them tools with the iron which were far superior to those they usually used. Being able to dress hides, Tom's family was soon dressed in fine leathern garments in place of the rawhide which formed their normal rough winter wear.

Genevera took to hunting with the bow and arrows which Jack had made for her. The two young people often hunted the moors of Morvah which were unoccupied in those days except for a kindly old giant, even older than Denbras had been, who lived amongst the rocks of Carne Galva. These hills were over run by herds of wild goats and sheep, deer and other game and wild animals. Genevra and Jack liked the downs and each other's company so much that they agreed that it would be pleasant to live up there by themselves. Jack thought that Tom, lord of a great castle and lands, might think a poor travelling tinkard too mean for his favourite daughter but he determined to ask for Tom's consent, for fashion's sake.

When Jack asked Tom for his daughter's hand, Tom readily agreed to the match.
"If I had the pick of the whole world and Market Jew besides, I should find no one I liked so much as thyself and I'll be bound that my old woman will say the same. What do'st say Joan?"
Joan was of the same mind as her husband.
"But what of the maid?" asked Tom.
"What do ee think she de spend so much of her time, braiding her hair and decking herself out with the gold and jewels for?" asked his wife "but to appear more fair in the tinker's eyes."

Tom built a dwelling for the pair, out on the hills and the whole family began to prepare for a grand wedding. Everyone in the castle worked hard on the new dwelling for Jack and Genevre but there was always time for play as well as toil. Quoits was a favourite game which Tom and Jack played in the castle yard. One wild throw resulted in a quoit stone landing on one of the sloping side of the castle where it broke through the turf covering and exposed the ground beneath. Tom was for replacing the turf and stamping it back into place but Jack's quick eye spotted something glittering beneath the turf.
"Look here!" he cried. There is tin here and rich stuff too." Jack dug down into the bank at the foot of the castle wall and found that it was entirely composed of glittering tin stone which the giants of old must have piled up there. The walls of the entire castle were lined with tin and then turfed over.
"What do we want with more of that trash?" cried Tom. "Haven't I told ee often enough that we have all that we could ever need here? Who could want more?"
"There is enough tin stone here" said Jack to his friend "to buy all the land between Hayle and Tol Pedn Penwith
"Half of it is mine already" said Tom. Leave the rest for others to squabble over."
"But just think, Tom booy" argued Jack "you are always saying that Joan's beer, good as it always is, cannot compare with the stuff your old master, Honey Chygwins brews in Market Jew. A sack full of this stuff would buy as much beer as we could need for the wedding. And all of it as strong as you like it best."

A strong leathern bag was soon filled with tin stone and, the next morning Jack and Tom Vean, Tom's eldest son, set out early for Market Jew. They sought Mayor Honey Chygwins, the brewer who was also the only tin smelter in that place at those times. King Chygwins was delighted to hear of his old servant Tom and how well he had got on in the world. He gave a fine opinion on the tin stone, declaring it to be of rich quality which would smelt into fine tin. He laughed when he heard that all that Tom wanted in exchange was a barrel of beer.
"I should want some rich stuff for Joan, Tom's wife, to make a gown fit for the lady of the castle" added Jack "and some more besides to make a fine dress for Genevre, his daughter who is to be my bride. The trouble is that I shall need someone to guide me in the choosing for I know little of women's fal-de-lalls."
King Hanibal Chygwins sent for his wife, Penelope (or Pee as he called her to save his breath), to help with the choosing of the cloth. That lady traded with

merchants visiting Market Jew from distant lands and seeking tin. Pee Chygwins had such a store of silks and brocade which amazed Jack the Tinkard and he was very glad that he had the Queen of Market Jew as a guide through this maze of splendours. Pee suggested four pieces to make as many dresses for Joan and Genevre. Two were of rich purple silk, flowered in gold for Joan and two were of clearest blue with silver sprigs of dainty needlework. Besides this fine fabric Jack took away many yards of ordinary cloth for common wear and several large shawls, so fine that they could be drawn through a finger ring. Pee thought of everything and the parcel contained gold and silver lace, thread and fastenings and even Pee's last new gown to act as a pattern.

The wainload of beer was sent off long before Jack was ready to start for home. Together with the bale of rich things, Pee sent her love to Joan and implored that the gowns be made in time for the smelting feast. Tom and his family had been invited to the next smelting-day to meet all the other fine folks who had rich stores of tin on their land. Jack had promised to return with more of the rich tin stone so that the next smelting-day would be the biggest ever held in Market Jew.

Tom Vean and Jack set off for home. The bale of fine things which Pee Chygwins had sent caused much joy, wonder and not a few tears in Tom's castle when it arrived. The family agreed that they should not despise everything outside the castle. A little fellowship with the rest of the world might add to their pleasures and content.

The next days were spent making sacks for tin stone and filling these, ready for the ox dray which Mayor Honey had promised to send to the castle. Tom accompanied the dray back to Market Jew when it was loaded because the road was very rough and stony. The sacks would fall off the wagon whenever it passed over the rocks and Tom's strength was needed to lift them back on, for tin stone weighs very heavy for its size and a sack was beyond the strength of most men. The Mayor was delighted to see his man, Tom, grown into a great lord and made him take so much of his finest drink that Tom could no longer stand and had to be tied onto the dray for the homeward journey. It was said that Tom could not even lie on the ground without holding on.

Honey Chygwins was so pleased with the great quantity of tin stone which Tom sent him over the next week but it made hardly a hole in the vast piles around

the walls of the castle. The purest of all, stream tin, stored in the castle caves was not even touched. On the first day of the feast, the castle was awake before dawn and all rushed down to the stream for their morning wash. They thought it best not to make too ostentatious a display so Joan only wore a few strings of amber and crystal over her robe of purple together with a bloodstone to protect against adders. Genevre was clad in the blue silk and she added a few strings of pearls and a couple of golden bracelets, studded with diamonds to make a modest show. As an afterthought she used a diamond circlet to fasten her silk gauze scarf against the breeze. The boys and men were dressed in new buff coats and the assembly made a grand show when the dray at last arrived to take them to Market Jew.

Joan and Genevre went straight into the hostelry, which was also the palace of Mayor Honey, and presented Penelope with some of the rarest jewels they had found in the giants' lockers. They were received with great ceremony and then led out to the tables spread beneath the oak trees where an assembly of noble lords and their ladies, the grand people of the district, were waiting. Included amongst these grand people were the lords of Godolphin and Pengursic. This latter was a very striking fellow indeed. He had a very swarthy complexion and was dressed very differently from his fellows with long flowing robes. Most striking of all were his eyes which were coal black and piercing. The lord of Pengursic had spent many years in the east, learning all that he could of the magical arts which have been practised there for many centuries.

After she had dined, Joan announced that she could hear her cows at Towednack, lowing to her and pleading to be milked and would have to return.

She gathered up all the children, all except Genevre who stayed behind with Jack the tinkard and Tom. The oxen were yoked to the wain and the Lady Penelope accompanied Joan and her brood as far as the foot of the hills. Soon, Joan and the children left the wain to lumber its way along the twisting road between the rocks. They could get on much faster, skipping over the carnes and taking a more direct route.

The lord of Pengursic seemed to have taken a particular liking to his new friend Tom and had drunk his health many times during the meal. Replying, as good manners demanded, to each toast, Tom drank deeply each time and was soon drunk and fell beneath the table to join the many others who had slipped there.

Joan milked her cows and put all the children to bed. By the time she took her supper outside to eat, the daylight had left the sky. She looked down on Market Jew with all its bright fires burning. There was firelight to be seen all round the bay even on top of The Mount. As Joan was surveying the festive scene, Genevre and Jack walked into the castle yard having let their horses loose onto the moors below.
"I'm glad to see you back" she called "but where's Tom? You should never have come home and left him with the conjurer. How often today have I wished that the tin had never been found. Who wouldn't rather be sitting here, dressed in homespun, eating barley bread and honey, drinking new milk at one's ease than be perched at a mayor's grand board, stiff as a stake, dressed in purple and afraid to move for fear of fousing the gay gown. Throw away the pearls, child and the amber, gold and crystal. They can never make thee more lovely than thou art with thy glossy black hair cascading down. Those gold bangles only burden thy arms. Hark to the dogs howling and the birds grieving for Tom. I would give ten times the tin to have Tom as content as he was a few weeks ago."
The Mayor's lady will see to Tom" Jack assured her. "She will give him a cordial and make sure he finds his bed."

Joan had seen how the fine ladies had admired Tom, his burly build, health and strength. She feared that Tom might be tempted by the flattery of one of these grand dames who might lead Tom off to a bed of her own. She feared this possibility even more than she feared the effect on Tom of any spells or potions of the Wizard of Pengursic. Joan, Genevre and Jack sat up late into the night before retiring and the sun was high in the sky before the lowing of the cattle woke Joan to the new day. At breakfast Joan said that she wished that the giants of old had left the tin in Trewe Bottom or in the Nancledra stream.
"I can't rest" she announced "for thinking of Tom, the great bucca, with more strength than sense, just like the giants, and how he was made drunk so soon by that crafty conjurer. He can drink gallon after gallon at home without becoming more stupid than usual. Surely the enchanter must have mixed some powder or potion in his drink. Neither Genevre nor I could look round to see what was afoot without encountering those piercing black eyes. I went from this castle very happy and proud but during the day I often wished myself home here in the hills once more."

In the drive over the moors, Penelope had told Joan of the wizard's powers and how he could raise the dead or the Devil with equal ease. Even Cormoran, the old giant of The Mount was afraid to show his face when the wizard was about. The old man, being hard up for food one day, waded across to the Pengursic fields and stole a bullock for his supper. The wizard bound him by magic, to a rock on his way back through the sea. The giant had to stand there all night with the bullock round his neck and the waves splashing in his face, nearly drowning him. In the morning the Wizard raised the spell and freed Cormoran, thinking him punished enough. Since that day the giant has caused no more trouble on the mainland. Other, more sinister things were said of the Wizard of Pengursic, that he could draw fire from the sun into a magic glass and use it to set the whole country ablaze. Some said that he employed the help of devils to make gold from clay and common stones. It was well known that the tower in the Wizard's castle was forbidden to all but the Wizard himself and one trusted servant. Fire and brimstone were seen burning there all day and all night.

"Go, Jack, my son" said Joan to the tinkard "and see what can be keeping Tom so long from his home. And don't come back without him."
"Speak of the devil and see his horns" said Jack as two horsemen were seen approaching the castle gate. "Behold our great bucca, Tom, bringing the enchanter into his castle. There is no mistaking the wizard's horse who hardly seems to tread on the ground. Some say it is no horse at all, but some devil he has broken in and bound to serve him."
"Genevre, child vean" said Joan, "keep to the room in the farther tower until I call you. I will prepare supper alone. Supper must be got for, if 'The Old One' himself came to the castle, one would be bound to treat him to the best cheer we had to offer."

Tom was obviously pleased with his visitor and showed him all the sheep and cattle in the lands around the castle. Jack was not at all well disposed towards the Wizard but could give no reason for his opinion. The visitor was so charming towards all of the castle inhabitants that eventually, even Jack warmed towards the great lord's easy courtesy. Joan and Genevre dressed themselves to show respect to their visitor and, for all his black reputation, when he entered the hall they could not admiring him for 'the handsomest man they ever saw, and bearing the air of a prince.'

However much Joan rejoiced to have Tom home again, she found herself charmed by the Lord of Pengersic. Whenever his gaze was directed towards Genevre or herself, the women felt spellbound like birds before an adder. The wizard tried the same trick on Jack the tinkard but his glances struck sparks off the hard look that Jack returned, like steel glancing off flint. Joan served the best supper she could assemble and a king would have been well satisfied with her hospitality. Healths were drunk in the best wines and the strongest beer by all the assembly except Jack. He would only accept the day-to-day brew to drink the toasts. At one point, Jack had to leave the hall and drive the wizard's steed away from the castle. The cattle and sheep returning from their pasture, would not enter their accustomed night time enclosure under the walls for fear of the beast. Even then they crowded round Tom's boys, trembling.

The Lord of Pengersic took up a harp but, before he began to play, he gave a shrill whistle which surprised the gathering and agitated the beasts in their enclosure afresh. This blast was followed immediately by such soothing music that the beasts outside, as well as the people within the castle were instantly made calm again. Even Jack began to relax a little. When all were comfortable once more, the wizard began to sing songs he had learned from his travels in the east. None but the minstrel could understand the words but gradually all began to nod and fall asleep beneath his musical spell. Jack, seeing the assembly beginning to nod, one after the other, slipped out to gauge the time by the disposition of the stars and the moon.
Outside in the courtyard he could see little but two shining points of light. Curious to find the source of these he moved closer until he could see that the wizard's steed had returned, summoned by the enchanter's whistle. Jack hurried back into the hall to find all asleep except the Lord of Pengursic who had cast aside his outer robe and stood clad in a gown covered with many magical figures. He wore a pentagram on a golden chain around his neck and he was waving a long slender rod over Joan, Tom and the rest. Wreaths of thick smoke swirled around the conjurer from a powder which he had thrown onto the fire.

Tom and Joan seemed as insensible as the stones on which they lay but Genevre, unable to speak or rise, stretched out her arms towards the tinkard. Jack tried to run to her aid but found that he had been effected by the poisonous vapour himself and stood, rooted to the spot. The Lord of Pengursic threw the helpless maid over his shoulder and started for the hall door. When he had left the castle, the wizard's influence waned slightly and Jack was able to follow him into the yard. He arrived in time to see the wizard and Genevre on the devil steed, galloping for the castle gate and leaving smoking hoof prints, each of which glowed blue for a short while after the hoof had left it. Jack grabbed for his bow and a quiver full of arrows.

In time of great danger, even the bravest of men will become as babes again and think upon their mothers. Jack's mother had bound a curious stone around his neck when he was a boy and explained that is was a talisman to keep him safe from witches, devils and any enchantments which might seek to harm him. Jack clutched the stone at his throat. It might have been magical power coming from the talisman itself or the miraculous power of a mother's love which caused Jack to feel an extra thrill of courage shoot through him and, following the hoof prints, he raced after the wizard.

At the gate, which the wizard's steed would normally have jumped with ease, the beast hesitated. Later it was suggested that the presence of an innocent maid on his back made the steed doubt his powers. Or perhaps Pengursic was unwilling to risk the maid when he saw the iron spikes which Jack had fixed to the top of the gate. Whatever the reason the wizard tried to open the gate, not realising that it was closed with a lock of Jack's own devising after the intrusion some months before. The wizard, for all his powers, was unable to loose the lock before Jack arrived and he howled with pain as an arrow pierced his right hand and nailed it to the wooden gate. The enchanter reached up his left hand to free its mate when the bow string twanged again and the other arm was pinned fast. Jack dropped the bow and grabbed for his tinker's hammer which always hung from his belt and he broke the wizard's arm with the first blow. The second blow broke the glittering star that adorned the brow of the wizard's steed and, as it shattered he cried for 'power from God above to help him overcome these demons from the pit of hell'. He tore Genevre from the saddle and laid her on the grass, senseless. Looking up, to ward off any further attack from either horse or rider, Jack only saw a large black adder slithering off under the gate and the wizard, seemingly shrunken in size at being deserted by his familiar, begging for mercy and to be released from the arrows.
"Beg all you like" cried Jack. "There you shall stay until I strip you of all your devil-spun toggery and my Genevre is fully restored."

Heavy blows from the hammer broke the circlet which bound the enchanter's brow and which glittered with jewels. Turning his weapon, he used the claw to wrench open the clasp of the wizard's cloak and then he tore off the girdle which he wore and which was adorned with further magical devices. His shirt

unbound, the gold and silver items hidden within and which the ungrateful guest had stolen, fell to the ground. When all trace of his magical apparatus had been removed, Jack struck off the iron arrow heads which bound the wizard to the gate, thus releasing the shrunken wretch who dropped to the ground and followed his steed under the gate. The dark, handsome, charming Lord of Pengursic, stripped of his devil's machinery, was now an old, ugly, withered, filthy, wretch who slunk away muttering threats and curses.
"Begone, wretch" said Jack. "I don't fear your curses and if you show your nose over the Towednack hills again I shall know how to deal with you. With my charmed stone and my hammer I defy every witch, wizard, conjurer and devil west of Carn Brea."

As soon as the wizard had gone, Jack sought to release Genevre from the wizard's spell. Remembering old tales and recipes which he had thought he would never need to use, he drew some pure, fresh water from the spring and dropped his charmed stone into it. He walked around Genevre, nine times against the sun, each time sprinkling her with the charmed well water. Gradually the maid regained her senses, whether from the effects of the spell or the shock of the cold water, who could tell? She called his name but was still under the effects of the wizards skills.
"Oh my dear Jack!" she murmured. "Take me away from this land of burning sun. The glitter of gold and crystal burn my eyes. Let me hide in thy bosom from the gaze of the enchanter. Take me back to my father's land, where the clouds hide the sun from time to time and we can have shade, peace and rest." When she opened her eyes and beheld her beloved's face close to hers, all thoughts of the wizard and his conjured visions fled and she slipped, this time into a peaceful sleep and all anxiety vanished from her face.

Jack next turned his thoughts to Joan, Tom and the others, still senseless on the slabs of the hall floor. He performed similar rites for the remaining victims of the wizard and, when they had either revived or had begun to snore normally he left them to care for each other. Jack had an important job of work to complete before the night was over. He gathered several faggots of furze together and set out for the castle gate. There he retrieved all of the devilish paraphernalia which he had stripped from the wizard before sending him slithering home to Pengursic. He made a fire of the furze and confined to its flames, all that he found polluting the ground by the gate. The fire burned fiercely and with many flashes and explosions as the devilish devices were destroyed. When the sun rose there was nothing but a blackened patch of earth to show where the purifying fire had raged in the night.

Whcn the castle folk awoke in the morning they felt stupefied, as though each had drunk too heavily the night before. Gradually all regained their usual vigour, all that is, except Tom who remained in very low spirits. In those far off days folk were seldom ill more than once in their lives and that sickness usually foretold their deaths. Sometimes in his delirium he raved about the enchanter and the fabulous sights that he had been promised while he was under the spell. At other times he spoke of the day they had spent with the Mayor of

Market Jew and all the great folk of West Cornwall. Finally, believing his death to be very close he asked for his mammy from Bowjeyheer in Ludgvan.

Tom's mammy was sent for and, when she came, she said that she wasn't at all surprised at how wealthy Tom had become, only how close to home he had found his fortune. The old lady was a wise woman, well respected in the district and able to tell the fortunes of all except herself. Joan cursed the tin as the cause of all the mischief.
"That all depends into who's hands it falls" Tom's mammy told her. "Tom should have kept out of bad company but, like other fools, he made feasts for wiser men to eat and only yesterday, thought a nod from a lord was as good as breakfast. Now, you go about your normal business while I tend to Tom and his tin. I shall soon cure the one and take care of the other. All that's wrong with Tom is high living and lazy times. His heart is clogged with fat. A few more days drinking Honey-The-Brewer's beer and it would be so weighed down as to be unable to move within his chest. Now Tom, you are to eat nothing but barley bread and drink nothing but vervain water or something else of your mammy's brewing for a week or two until your big belly is reduced to a healthy handsome size and you can go about your hedging again. I shall kill ee or cure ee my son, for just now, thou art no use in life and naught but a trouble to yourself and all about ee."

Tom followed his mammy's advice and guidance and recovered his health, strength and spirit. The old lady lived with Tom and Joan in the castle from that time onwards and kept Tom healthy and made sure the tin was only disposed of to get more land for the boys in the growing family of Tom and Joan of Towednack.

Jack and Genevre were married at the beginning of August and moved into a stone built dwelling in Morvah to raise a large family. The dwelling was enlarged several times over the years, to accommodate the growing numbers. They eventually became so numerous and famous that a three acre field was needed to hold all the family members who gathered together each August to celebrate Jack and Genevre's anniversary. It was from these high country boys, Jack of the Hammer and Tom the Hedger, that many of the great Cornish families are descended. The wedding celebrations are still held on August Sunday each year. More recently, they have become known as Morvah Fair.

Tom Trenoweth's Pig

Tom was a cousin of Betty Trenoweth, she whom folks believed to be a witch because she had cursed Madam Noy and the curse had come true. One Thursday in the Spring of the year, and unknown to each other, both cousins had come from St Buryan to Penzance market, each to buy a pig to fatten for winter.

It took Betty nearly two hours to walk the five miles to market so, when she eventually arrived, there was but one pig left for sale. Betty began to bargain with the seller. After half an hour there were only a few pence between the seller's price and what Betty would offer. Betty tried a trick that had worked in the past and walked away, intending to saunter back a short while later, pretending to be no longer interested in the bargain. Few buyers remained at the market and the seller might want to sell at Betty's price, rather than go back home with his pig.

No sooner had Betty left, than Cousin Tom appeared and bought the pig at a little more than Betty was offering. Betty returned and found Tom, tying a rope to the pig's leg, ready to take it home to Buryan.

"What you doin' with my pig, Tom?" asked Betty.

"She idn' yours Betty. I just bought her" said Tom.

"And what made you interfere when I was in price for the sow?" asked Betty. "If I don't have her then thee shall wish thy cake dough and find her the dearest bargain thou hast ever had."

"The pig is mine, Betty Trenoweth" said Tom. "Bought and paid for and I aren't givin' her up."

Betty repeated the ritual which had done so much damage to Madam Noy, mumbling to herself, pointing and shaking her finger at Tom. Tom expected a curse but he was wrong. Betty turned her attention on the pig and bent down to whisper in the animal's ear. Tom jerked on his rope and walked off with the pig. As soon as he got her home, he put her in the crow and filled her trough with swill and locked her in for the night.

The next morning, Tom found the crow door open and the sow rooting in his neighbour's garden, doing no end of damage. It took the efforts of all Tom's friends in St Buryan to drive the pig back into the crow but next day she was gone again, even though Tom had taken great care when fastening the door. In the months which followed, the pig ate all the corn, milk and meal that Tom gave her but remained as skinny as she was on the day when Tom bought her. She continued to escape each night and cause damage for which Tom had to pay.

One day Betty called and asked "Well Tom, how is thy sow? Will she be fat against Christmas? I hear she is very troublesome. Perhaps you had better sell her to me. What do ee look for her now?"

Tom dug in his heels. "If she idn' fat for seven years of Sundays you shain't profit for begrudging her to me, black old witch that you are. I'll drive her to Penzance and sell her for less than I gave for her rather than you shall have her."

Over the months that followed Betty called several times to enquire after the pig and each time offered less than she had offered previously. The pig became thinner at every visit and soon would be skin and bone. Eventually, one Thursday, Tom tied a rope to the pig's leg once more and started to drive her to market in Penzance to sell her and minimise his loss. The rivers were flowing more strongly than they had been in the spring time and the pig now refused to cross the first torrent that they encountered at Bejewyan Bottoms. Tom grabbed her hind legs and tried to make her cross, wheel-barrow fashion. The frightened animal wriggled and kicked and twisted between Tom's legs and ran off over hedges and ditches with Tom in hot pursuit. The sow tired after a while and slowed so that Tom could step on her rope. He sat down looking like a boutigo in his clothes, torn to rags by coursing after the pig through the brambles and furse. To ensure that he didn't let the pig loose again, Tom tied the rope to his wrist.

"Late as it is" said Tom, "I shall get ee to Penzance market yet". As he spoke a hare lept out of a bush and squeeked a tiny 'chee-ah' before sprinting away. Now 'chee-ah' is the noise you make when calling a pig and Tom's pig responded to the sound and sped after the hare, pulling Tom off his feet and dragging him after her. The hare disappeared into a drain which ran under the road and the skinny pig followed where Tom was too stout to go. There Tom lay, in the ditch, beside the road with one arm down the drain, still tied to the pig. The drain was obviously a comfortable resting place because the pig gave no signs of wanting to move from it.

With his left hand, Tom managed to take his knife from his pocket and, with great difficulty, managed to cut himself free. Tom sat by the drain for a long while, trying to pursued the pig out of the hole. Eventually who should appear on the road but Betty Trenoweth, clicking her knitting needles as she walked, making herself a stocking. "Is that you, cousin?" she asked, feigning surprise. "Have ee sold the sow and got drunk on the profit, that you are lying in the ditch?"

"Well cousin Betty," said Tom, "I must say as how thou hast bested me. The pig is in the drain and she won't come out. But then you de knaw that already for I b'lieve it was you that jumped out of the bush and called the pig after ee. Thy friend the Devil lent ee the power to change thyself into a hare, I s'pose?"

"As you're a cousin of mine, Tom" said the old woman, "I shall forgive ee the blasphemin' lies you're a tellin', and I shall give ee the value of your pig if you will sell 'er to me. And that's half of what you give for 'er in the Spring of the year for she has gone to skin and bone in your care, seem te me."

"I'll take it, damn yer eyes, so long as you give me a bite to eat as well, for I haven't tasted a mossle all day" said Tom. Betty paid the price and gave Tom a loaf that she had in her basket. Next she put her mouth to the mouth of the drain and called softly "chee-ah, chee-ah" and the pig strolled calmly out of the hole and followed Betty all the way home to Buryan like a dog.

Tom took the money to the Bird in Hand at Sancreed where he stayed for as long as the cash lasted. As he said; "if I de lay it by, every shillin' of the devil's money will go and take nine more with it." Betty kept the pig as a store-sow for many years and it became the parent of a prodigious family.

This tale is often told about Maggy Figgy, the witch of St Levan, instead of Betty Trenoweth. Maggy Figgy was an altogether more substantial witch than Betty and it was said of her that she conjured storms by witchcraft to drive ships onto the rocks below Maggy Figgy's chair, near the Lands End. Hoards of lesser witches would prey upon the victims of these shipwrecks and then fly off on bunches of ragwort to visit other sorcerers in Wales. The style of magic in this story is much less malicious than that attributed to Maggy Figgy.

The Watcher

Madron Carn is a peaceful place and an excellent vantage point. From the top of the pile of boulders you can see the whole sweep of Mount's Bay from The Lizard right around to Penlee Point. There is a fine painting in Penlee House Gallery in Penzance which shows the view from the Carn as it was a couple of hundred years ago. That view must be very similar to the view seen by Merlin in the days of King Arthur.

Even in my school days the vista was less cluttered and the carn itself was much more open than it is today. Cattle grazed there and used to scratch themselves contentedly on the menheir, or standing stone, just south of the carn. These days they just have to put up with the itch because the menheir is long gone. There was a wood to the west of the carn and the gardens of Trengwainton to the south west. We boys would often play in the wood, climbing the trees and making camps. Sometimes we might climb the stone pile of the carn instead and when we were tired we would simply lie in the sunshine and stare at the clouds or at the wonderful view. On the edge of the wood, to the Northwest, there was a cave. It was low and blackened from years of camp-fires. You could sit in there and imagine that you were occupying the same space that witches used, long years before, for casting spells and mixing potions.

There was always something to do 'up Madron Carn' and the something which we did more than anything else was playing hide and seek. Around the carn there was a mixture of rabbit grazed lawn, rock and furze cover which was excellent for the game. Madron hide and seek was no trivial affair where, after five minutes or so, "two, four, six, eight" saved the lot and declared the game to be over. Our games were serious and went on for hours. We usually played in pairs, hunting each other so that each player was both hider and seeker at the same time.

The carn is still a magical place but it is so overgrown with furze, bramble and rhododendron now that much of the space we enjoyed as boys is now inaccessible. Cattle no longer keep the place open by grazing. The wood has gone, killed by Dutch elm disease or strangled by rhododendron. I can't find the witches cave any more. Even the carn itself is threatened by choking undergrowth. Hide and seek can't be anywhere near such good fun as it was in our days.

If you stand at the summit of the carn and walk towards the western precipice then you are close to The Watcher. Look north along the edge of the rocks and, if you are at all romantic and imaginative then you will see a giant's head looking westward, towards the Scillies. You might say that he's asleep and it is true that he never moved in all the hours that I sat and watched him. But he's not asleep! You can tell from the keen, searching look on his face that he has kept his vigil faithfully for many hundreds of years. What he watches for has not yet come to pass.

The Watcher was set on the carn by Merlin, the wizard of King Arthur's court, to watch for a magical happening. For, once upon a time, long, long ago, while King Arthur ruled, it was said that a goodly land named Lethowsow or Lyonesse, extended beyond what we now know as the Land's End and stretched as far as the Scilly Isles. The land of Lyonesse was believed to have been rich and fertile and to have supported many families, large flocks and herds. Some say that there were no fewer than forty churches to be found there. They also say that King Arthur ruled in Lyonesse.

Wherever Arthur was ruling at the time of the events which I am describing, his reign was drawing to a close. Treason had thinned the ranks of the famous Knights of the Round Table. Sir Kaye remained true, together with Sir Caradoc, Sir Tristram and Sir Lancelot of the Lake but there were many empty seats around Arthur's table. Prince Mordred's chair was vacant and it was rumoured that Mordred would soon declare open war on Arthur, his royal cousin and benefactor.

One night, while Arthur sat in his hall with his knights around him and his queen, Guinevere by his side, Arthur's mood was troubled. Minstrels played and sang as usual but there was a want of the free-hearted courtesy and confidence the company had enjoyed in former days. Still, the semblance of good-fellowship was kept up until the time came for the King to retire. Taking up a golden cup to pledge his guests, Arthur surveyed the company. A shudder passed through his frame when his eye rested on Mordred's seat for the chair seemed not to be empty. A strange, indistinct, shadowy form rested there.

"The great wizard Merlin is among us,"

cried the King "and there will be evil in the coming days. Break up the court! This is not a time for feasting, but rather for fasting and for prayer."

On the following day, word of Mordred's revolt reached the castle. Day after day, news came of fresh foes, flocking to the rebel standard. Mordred's army increased as it advanced but, strangely, Arthur showed no inclination to ride out and meet the traitor. Had his brave heart quailed at last? Had his good sword Excalibur lost its magic virtue? Some thought that he doubted the fidelity of those who still remained about him. He kept within his castle until the rebels approached to the very gates. This strange silence on the part of the King unsettled his enemies who had time to ponder the fact that they were about to match themselves against warriors who had grown old in fellowship with Victory!

When the main body of the invaders stood outside Camelot, the great castle bell rang out and the trumpets called the faithful knights to horse. King Arthur, his knights and men at arms, the best warriors of Britain, arose and rode out to fight their final battle against a much larger foe.

The few who remained at the end of the day were in no condition to offer further fight to Mordred or any other foe. They carried Arthur's torn banner, still wet with the King's blood and fled unwillingly, not knowing how to conduct themselves, being so unused to retreat. They headed for Lyonesse, dashing over the bleak moors without uttering a word. Thirty miles they rode that day, hard pressed by the vindictive Mordred and his army, thundering after them. The broken knights took what rest they could when night fell and riding was no longer possible. In the morning, they rode on once more with Mordred in merciless pursuit.

By mid morning, Mordred was less than a mile behind Arthur's fleeing knights who, unwilling to be dragged down by the renegade's hounds, pulled up their mounts with a plan of facing their foe and selling their lives dearly. They gazed sternly on the advancing host when, all at once, a mist rose up between the two forces. It was a strange shadowy mist, without distinct form. Sir Caradoc saw a resemblance between this fog and the strange form which had occupied Mordred's chair on Arthur's last night at the round table. He remembered the King's words on that occasion.
"It is Merlin, the Great Wizard" cried the knight.

Slowly the cloud rose between the pursuers and pursued and Mordred's army was engulfed in its murk. Arthur's knights had, by this time, crossed the plane of Lyonesse and were climbing the last hills which marked the place where the land gave

way to the great Atlantic Ocean. Suddenly a terrible change occurred in the atmosphere, which became oppressive and sultry. Low, muttering thunder accompanied strange heavings of the earth beneath Mordred's horse's hooves. At the same time the cloud gradually condensed in front of Mordred himself and assumed the form of Merlin the Wizard. For a few seconds the two stood, face to face, frowning on each other in awful silence. Then Merlin raised his arm, and immediately the thunder increased and the earth began to undulate and rend as if the very foundations of the world were destroyed. Great fissures appeared, and the rocks welled up like the waves of the sea. With a cry of dismay, Mordred's army turned to fly. But it was too late. Already the earth was rent into fragments; it heaved convulsively for a few seconds more and then sank beneath the level of the deep. The ocean rushed in wildly, leaving nothing behind to mark the spot where land had been, save the Lyonesse hills which we now know as The Scilly Isles.

The people of Lyonesse fled before the two armies. Most headed for the western hills, afraid of the consequences of becoming trapped between the two forces. Only one rider, by name of Trevellian, rode his horse east and kept just ahead of the flooding ocean as it drowned the land behind him. He rode towards the higher land, now called Tol Pedn in Penwith, and gained his objective just as the sea arrived to batter the cliffs of the Land's End as it has done ever since.

Now! You may believe my story or not as you choose but remember that the land of Cornwall has unquestionably given up part of its soil to the sea. St. Michael's Mount was formerly known as Careg Cowes in Clowse or 'a hoar rock in a wood' and was described as lying 'some miles from the sea'. Today The

Mount is an island except at low tide when it may be reached by a causeway. On Marazion beach, when I was a boy, only sixty years ago, you could see the trunks of the trees sticking out of the sand when the tide was out. Similar trunks were to be seen at Tolcarne in Newlyn. Further evidence of the sea overwhelming the land can be seen as you walk back to Penzance from Tolcarne. At low water you will see the foundation stones of the road which formerly linked the two towns. These stones are today far below the high water line. To keep dry at all states of the tide today you must travel along The New Road, a hundred yards inland

Details change as stories are passed from teller to listener and again, when that listener becomes the teller in his turn. Trevellian was reported by some to have landed at Whitsand Bay and not Tol Pedn in Penwith. Some even say that he rode out of the surf at Perranuthnoe, twenty miles away. Who is to say now, which story is the real story of the death of Arthur? Some scholars report that Arthur defeated Mordred in battle but was mortally wounded in the process. He died requesting that his sword, Excalibur, be cast into a lake. When his wish was fulfilled, Excalibur was caught up by a ghostly hand rising out of the waters. Some say that he will come again and retrieve his sword. And I say, that is why Merlin placed his watcher, high on Madron Carn, looking ever westward, waiting for the land to rise again with a reborn Arthur, the once and future king, riding out of Lyoness to claim his sword from the waters of Gwavas Lake.

Nelly Wearne

"What is that maid like?" asked Amelia Warren.
"What's who like?" enquired Peter, her husband.
"That Nelly Wearne" replied Amelia.
"She? She's a 'ansome maid she is, pretty as a pickchur and lively as a colt" announced Peter.
"Ess" was Amelia's somewhat sarcastic response to her husband's opinion. "She's lively all right and I grant that she's a fitty young maid but that don't excuse nothin'."
"What's there to excuse?" asked Peter, surprised by the vehemence of Amelia's tone. "She haven't done nothin' to you have she?"
"There's a brear lot to excuse, even before last night!" declared Amelia. She had obviously been privy to some special intelligence, carried to the cottage while Peter was busy in the cowshed, doing the morning milking. "She de bring shame on the whole of Buryan Church Town with her gallivanting" she continued. "And the tongue on her, my soul!"

Peter Warren was not as inclined as his wife to seek out news of their neighbours' doings nor to express opinions about their characters but he would tolerate no insult to either Amelia or himself. "What have she said to ee then?" he asked. "Leave me knaw and I'll have a word with Squire Cardew."
"And what's he goin' to do?" demanded Amelia. "Everybody do knaw ee's her faither, even if she is s'posed to be a maid up to Squire's house. She's spoilt rotten she is. No wonder she de behave like she do. Squire wain't have a word said again' her and she's allowed to run wild. She'll only help Madam Cardew, if she feel like it and she's off like a hare if she de find somethin' more to her likin'."

Nelly Wearne's station in society was not at all uncommon. Gentlemen landowners were wont to produce illegitimate offspring, sometimes in alarming numbers. These children were seldom openly acknowledged by their fathers but it was felt that their parentage should confer some social advantage on them. Such children were usually found a place within the gentleman's household or

an apprenticeship with a trusted employee. Nelly was appointed to assist the Squire's mother, Madam Cardew, to keep house for her son. In spite of Nelly's lack of enthusiasm for the work, Madam Cardew was very fond, even a little proud, of the handsome, spirited, young girl.

Peter Warren, assured that no insult had been delivered by Nelly, returned to his defence of the young woman. "She's a young maid, and the handsomest for miles around and the best dancer by far. What do ee expect?" he told his wife. Peter obviously expected that these qualities of Nelly's far outweighed her disinclination to carry out hum-drum household chores.
"Trust you to take her side" complained his wife. "That's men all over that is. Don't matter how she de behave herself. If she de flash they eyes at ee and show ee a bit of ankle when she's disportin' of herself on the dance floor, you don't think of all the work she left for poor Madam Cardew to do back home."
"In are ee?" cried a newcomer to the kitchen from the doorway. Zelda Harvey had come visiting. Amelia's kitchen was an important centre for the exchange of news in St Buryan, situated as it was close to the conjunction of several well used paths into the town place. Zelda had first hand news about the goings on at the celebrations of St Buryan Feast and she was finding it increasingly uncomfortable to keep it within herself.
"Come on in, Zelda my dear and have a dish of tea will ee" cried Amelia. "Have ee heard about Nelly Wearne at the feast last night?"
"Heard about her!" exclaimed the excited visitor. "My gar! I was there and seen it with me own eyes. And I just been up to the Squire's kitchen and seen Madam Cardew herself. It was she that told me what happened before Nelly arrived at the feast. It seems that Madam had told Nelly that she couldn't go to the dance last night. Squire had been entertaining and there was too much for Madam to do all on her own and anyway, that storm had been brewing all afternoon."
"That didn't please the maid, I imagine" suggested Amelia.
"Please her!"cried Zelda. "Madam Cardew is still smartin' from the tongue lashing that she got from Nelly when she told her she had to stay home. She de get it from her faither. You don't want to get on the wrong side of ee if you can help it, do ee Peter?"
"Squire's all right if you de treat un all right" declared Peter who didn't like to get drawn into discussions where he was obliged to criticise his landlord. Zelda ignored his careful reply.
"And if you de get on the wrong side of un" she continued, "then he de bawl and rant at ee 'til you feel like you been kicked by the bull. And Nelly's just as bad."

Amelia was well aware of the strength of character of the squire and his daughter but here was an eye witness! What she really wanted to hear was the

full story of what had happened the night before and with as many details as possible.
"Will ee tell us what happened Zelda?" she pleaded. "I only heard that Nelly arrived at the dance, wet leakin' from the rain storm. Old Jan Hocking told me that there was ruckshuns as soon as she came in."
"Ruckshuns wadn' in it my dear!" said Zelda. "Madam Cardew told me that Nelly said there wasn't nobody on earth who could stop her dancing at the feast. She just put up her best gown, stormed out of the house and over the fields just as the rain started. There was fire in her eyes when she burst into the Inn."
"I s'pose the lads crowded round hoping for a dance with the hussy as soon as she arrived" said Amelia..
"True enough" said Zelda "but Nelly wadn' havin' none of they. Told them they were all clod hoppers she did, and that she would only dance with a man who could match her, step for step.
"Would you credit the boldness?" said Amelia, "To storm off to the dance leaving others to do your work and then insult all the young men of the town. I s'pose she stormed out in a fit of temper after that. I hear tell she haven't been seen since."
"Not she my dear" said Zelda."The lightning was flashing by then but there was something else that stopped Nelly from storming from the room."
"What was that then Zelda?" asked Peter, curious in spite of himself, to hear the story which had so excited the two women.
"The door flew open and in walked a man the like of which you never saw in all your life" announced Zelda dramatically. "Ee was dressed in a black suit of fine clothes with white lace up to his neck and sprouting from his cuffs. He had a great black hat with a white feather in it. And there was a great silver cutlass hanging from his belt and rings to his fingers and a jewelled pin in his cravat and silver buckles and ..."
Peter interrupted her "Sound like a real dandy don't uh 'Melia?"
"Not he, Peter" was Zelda's grave reply. She had obviously been mightily impressed by the newcomer the night before, as had the rest of the company. "There wadn' a man in the place who would speak a word to un unless he was asked to. The Captain was a prince amongst men and no mistake. The room was held silent, just by his standing there. He seemed to cast a spell on all of us."
"What happened next, my dear?" asked Amelia impatiently. Zelda resumed her account of the preceding evening's drama.
"The only thing that moved in the room was the captain's eyes as he surveyed the company. And they only moved until they fell upon Nelly Wearne. She was still wet leaking from the storm but the Captain picked her out from all the other maids in their finery. He walked straight up to Nell and said to her 'will you honour me with a dance my fine, pretty maid?'

"What did she say to un, Zelda?" asked Peter, caught up in the story now, every bit as much as his wife was.

Zelda continued. "The honour will be mine sir" was all she said. And then the Captain spoke to his companion who no one had noticed until that moment. 'Bosun' he said, 'will you give us the good old tune?' The bosun took a small pipe from a pocket in the tail of his coat and he cried out in a loud voice 'a floor! a floor for Captain Black and the lovely Nell.' And then the bosun started to blow, quietly at first. Captain Black bowed to Nelly who curtsied in reply and the two began to dance to the bosun's pipe."

"And did the fiddlers and pipers from the town join in the tune?" asked Peter.

"Not they" Zelda replied. "All eyes were fixed on the splendid Captain Black and the lovely Nelly Wearne. Such steps as they danced had never been seen before in Buryan not even from Nelly herself at earlier dances. No dancer dared to show his poor counterfeit of such dancing. And no fiddler dared to offer his poor scrapings to be compared to the magical music which the bosun breathed from his pipe. All watched as the wonder unfolded and swelled before them. The bosun's measure was slow and melancholy at first. Then, after a while the bold captain called out 'Faster if you will, bosun. And faster still for I have never danced with such a maid as my sweet Nell.' Soon the tune was flying from the pipe at a wild pace and other revellers from other rooms in the Church Town crowded into the ball room of the Inn to watch the marvel that was Nelly Wearne and Captain Black, dancing to the wild piping of Ackie Carne, the Captain's bosun."

"What, the whole town, in that small room?" asked the astonished Peter Warren.

"Indeed so" declared Zelda. "and the space left for Nelly and Captain Black was

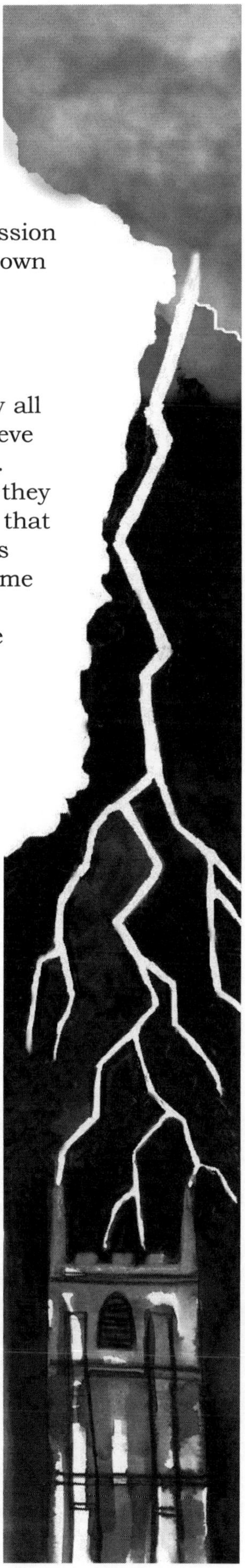

all too cramped for the extravagance of their steps so the Captain motioned to the bosun to lead the dancing pair out of the ballroom and into the square before the Church to explore yet more daring steps and leaps. Soon the whole town was formed into a procession with Nelly, the Captain and his piper at the head and the rest of the town following and now daring to join in with steps of their own."
"But waddn' it raining all night?" asked Amelia "Ee was here wadn' it, Peter?"
"Rain, thunder and lightning all night seem me" answered Peter.
"Nobody seemed to notice the rain, nor the thunder" said Zelda. "They all danced like they was possessed and soon enough folks started to believe they *was* possessed and that Captain Black was no sea captain at all. Some said that when the Captain leaped high in the air with Nelly as they capered you could see a tail hanging beneath his coat. Some believed that the Captain had bewitched the town with his dancing and that he was none but the Old One himself and Ackie Carne was his Beelzebub, come to drag them all off to Hell. And some of the town's folk started to fall away from the dance and creep off home. But others danced on, more wildly with every flash of lightning and every clap of thunder.

And then someone with more presence of mind than all the others, entered the church and started to toll the bell to disperse the storm. Soon after the first ringing stroke from the tower, there was one more vivid flash of lightning and monstrous clap of thunder, so close upon each other that you could not separate the two. As folks recovered their hearing after this blast from the sky they noticed that the piping had stopped and that Nelly, the Captain and his bosun were nowhere to be seen."
"Had they been struck by the lightning?" asked Peter.
"No" declared Zelda, "they had disappeared from the face of the earth. The people became wild when they noticed what had happened and some seem to have lost their wits for they ran about the town square and into and out of the churchyard, screaming. Old Mrs Quick is still raving so I am told and may have to be sent to Bodmin asylum if she doesn't recover soon."
"Well, what happened then Zelda?" asked Amelia.
"I don't know, my 'ansomes" replied Amelia sadly.
"You dunno!" exclaimed Amelia and Peter in unison.
"No, my dears" said Zelda. "My Josiah, you know how much of a church man he is, he grabbed me by the arm and rushed me off home and wouldn't leave me look back, not once! 'Siah said as how there was Devil's business goin' on in Burryan last night and we shouldn't allow ourselves to get caught up in it. I was hopin' there might be someone here who might have heard the end of the story. That's why I come visitin' this mornin'. Seem te me the lot of us shall have to wait a bit more before we get to hear the end of the tale."

The Witchy Wood

Walking in the Witchy Wood.
Mother doesn't know.
She told me "take the long way round"
But that would be so slow.

I didn't mean to stay so long.
I know I left too late.
And now I'm in the darkest dark,
So far off from the gate.

What was that? Was it a bat?
A bear? Or something bigger?
It made a noise, a sort of squelch
Or was it more a slither?

Slither! What if it's a snake?
All coils and poison dripping!
What if it's a vampire?
My blood he'll soon be sipping!

Oh why did I go through this wood?
I know its reputation.
It frightens me and gives me such
A horrible sensation.

What was that? Was that my name?
Who could know me here?
Is it a ghost, a ghoul or worse?
It's nothing good, I fear.

The Witchy Wood

I can't get out. I've lost the path.
It knows my name. I've had it.
My number's up. I've had my chips.
I'm just a frightened rabbit.

Where can I hide? The moon's come out.
There's nowhere it can't find me.
My name again! It's got a light
To find me with. Cor blimey!

I cannot look and yet again
I must know what it looks like.
There it is. It's nearer now.
A witch! Her nose quite hook like.

It ***is*** a witch, that pointy hat
And horrid green hair flying.
It screeches out my name again.
I'm sure I'll soon be dying.

My heart is bumping in my chest.
My blood is surging madly.
The only way that this can end
For me is rather badly.

The witch is almost on me now.
I trip. I fall. She's caught me.
"Are you alright? Hope you're not hurt."
The hag? She's my friend, Courtney!

"It's Halloween, you twit" she said.
"You're coming to my party.
If you're not hurt, go home and change
Then back to mine, real smartly."

Written to celebrate Halloween
at Newlyn School.

Gold and Silver

You boys are nearly men" their mother told them. "You must go out, into the world, and make your own fortunes for your poor dead father was unable to leave you any birthright."

"I shall make a great fortune of gold" said her son with yellow hair, "for my hair is golden, just as my father's was. But you must give me a little gold before I go, Mother, to start me on my way."

"My dear son" said his mother, "you shall have all the gold that I possess but I fear that little remains." And she went to her store room, soon to return with a small bag and a long face. "All I can give you, my dear son, is this bag of worthless, golden grains."

The boy took the bag and looked within.
"Do not despair, Mother", cried her first born son. "I will strive to make our fortune or die in the attempt."

The sadness on his mother's face deepened as she heard his words.
"How can you make a fortune from such poor stuff as I have to give you? And even if you could, how long would it take, my dear boy?" asked his mother.
"One hundred days" cried the boy. "In one hundred days I shall return enough

gold to repay your kindness mother and more besides for you, for me and for my brother, for the rest of our days."
"How will you do this, my son? How will you make your small bag of gold grow so, in just one hundred days?"
"Have faith in me mother" her son replied as he walked from the house "and faith will be rewarded."

The lady turned to her second son, he with hair as black as pitch. His mother too, wore raven hair when her second son was born but now the black was touched, here and there, with silver.
"What fortune will you make my son?" she asked.

"I shall make a fortune of silver mother" the boy replied. "Have you any silver for me to help me start my quest?"

"My dear son, I have no silver in my store" said his mother, distressed at having nothing to offer to her second son. "Indeed, little of anything remains and I fear that we shall starve before your brother returns with his golden fortune in a hundred days."
"Do not despair, mother" cried the black haired, younger boy. "Only look in the store room and see what might remain to help me."

The mother went once more to her store room and when she returned she was weeping, for all that remained was a ball of twine. She showed her son the string.

"Give it to me mother and I will do my best to make it serve. Have faith and pray that I succeed."
"I will pray as you ask" said the mother "but I believe that I shall starve and die before either you or your brother return."
"Dear mother," said her son, "I shall not

need a hundred days. I shall find my silver fortune sooner than my brother finds his of gold. We will survive and we will prosper, all three of us."

The second son walked out of the house with his mother to join his brother on the cliff above the sea. Their mother embraced her sons and bade them farewell.

"We shall not go far, mother" said the golden son.
"We will find our fortunes here" said his brother.
"There is no fortune here, my boys" their mother replied. "Riches must be sought from far afield."

As the two brothers walked from the house to the sea, the golden boy scattered the grains of gold from his mother's bag onto the earth. His dark haired brother knotted his string into a web which he cast into the sea. The dark boy drew in his web from the waves and, tangled within it was silver. Many silver fishes. And day after day the web was cast and, more often than not, silver fishes were caught.

The golden boy was content to watch his gold turn slowly, oh so slowly, to green. He watched his green grow in the sunshine and the rain. As the green grew, the breeze blew billows through it, mocking the waves on the sea below. For one hundred days it grew until, once more it turned to gold. On the hundredth day the golden boy cut his corn and poured his golden grain into bags. He placed most of his harvest in his mother's store room but some he sold. With the money he made by selling golden grain in the market, he bought more twine for his brother. The younger son wove an even larger web and, with this, he fished for more fishes in the silver sea.

The gold and silver brothers prospered and their mother rejoiced in her sons. There was grain enough for bread all winter and, in the springtime of the following year, there were several bags of gold remaining in the store. Once more, the golden boy cast the golden grains upon the earth and while they burst and grew, his brother drew forth many a silver harvest from the sea. As time passed and the cycle repeated, the boys grew into fine men. The gold and silver sons married wives who brought forth sons and daughters of their own. For many years the sons, and the sons of sons, enjoyed fresh fortunes of gold and silver.

Selena Moor

You remember Madam Noy, she who battled with Betty Trenoweth and lost? Well, this is the story of one of her kinfolk, William. Madam Noy was a mean, vindictive old spite of a woman but there is good and bad in most families and William might have been placed on this earth simply to balance the Noys' account.

William and some of his men were helping his cousins, the Pendars of Baranhual, on the day before the gulthise, or 'harvest home'. The company realised that more help would be needed if the harvest was to be gathered in time. After the croust break that morning, Mr Noy left for St Buryan to fetch more hands. William was diligent and, by nightfall, he had gathered a good number of workers to complete the work on the next day. His job done, Mr. Noy and his dog left the Inn at Buryan and set off for Baranhual once more. When he did not arrive, Dame Pendar was not unduly worried for she believed that William must have gone to his own home at Pendrea for the night.

For all his popularity, William Noy was all alone in the world. There had been romance in his life but his intended bride had died suddenly some years before and he had never sought love again. There was no one to notice that he had not arrived at his own home. When, the next day, the harvesters gathered at Baranhual, neither sight nor sign of William Noy was reported by anyone in the company. The most likely reason for his absence, that he had gone to help a neighbour even more in need than Dame Pendar, was accepted. Soon William Noy was driven from everyone's minds by the arrival of hasty pudding for breakfast and news of apple pie later. Beer and cider kept him from their thoughts for the remainder of the day, until the last truss of corn had been cut and the ancient ceremony of 'Crying the Neck' had been enacted.

Before all the roast beef, mutton, squab pie, rabbit and hare pie, puddings and other substantial fare had been served, Dame Pendar sent out messengers to find Mr. Noy and bring him to the feast. All returned without any tidings. The next day a search began in earnest for now his friends feared for William's safety. All the pools, streams, cliffs and other dangerous places were examined but there was no sign of the missing man. On the second day after gulthise, searchers were sent further afield, into neighbouring parishes, for Mr. Noy was well liked everywhere and hunted regularly with neighbouring packs. It was on the third day after the feast that a horse was heard neighing and a dog barking on a piece of dry ground almost surrounded by bogs and pools on the Pendrea side of Selena Moor. No one had thought of looking for Mr Noy in a place so close to his home.

After much trouble, a way through the treacherous mire was found and the searching party stepped onto the dry island where they found Mr. Noy's horse and hound. The horse had found grazing enough for himself but the poor dog looked famished. Nevertheless, it was this animal which led the searchers through the thicket to an old ruined bowjey which no one had known was to be found there. In the winter, the land was considered too wet and tretcherous for anyone to attempt a crossing. In warmer weather, the land was choked with thorns and brambles and, like all such places, it was swarming with adders.

The dog scratched the ground near the drushell of the bowjy but would not cross it. When the searchers entered the building they found William Noy lying fast asleep on the ground. Waking the sleeper was difficult and, when he did finally opened his eyes, he was astonished at what he saw.
"Why, 'tis all my friends from Baranhual and Pendrea! What are you all doing so far from home?"
No one attempted to answer his bewildering question. A brandy bottle was produced and the poor man was dosed, lifted gently to his feet and helped to mount his horse. The animal carried him out of the bog and then to his home, accompanied by his rescuers. Throughout the journey, William Noy seemed amazed to find himself in his own country for he believed that he had ridden many miles from home.
"No matter" cried William when he crossed the stream and rode onto his own estate. "I shall rest a little today so as to be ready for gulthise tonight."
"My dear man" said one of the party "gulthise was three days ago. We been lookin' for ee ever since."

William could not believe what he had been told and thought that his rescuers were playing a prank upon him. It was only later, when he was shown the ricks and the sacks of grain and all the harvest tools oiled and put away until next year that he began to believe what he was being told. When he was sitting in his own kitchen again and his breakfast was being prepared he asked his friends to sit while he tried to tell them what had befallen him.

William had intended to return to Baranhual after his stay in St Buryan and took a short cut across Selena Moor. The horse, used to choosing his own way back from the inn, wanted to take the high road. The conflict of intentions between horse and rider took the pair out of their way and they were soon lost. As soon as William realised his predicament he tried retracing his steps but to no avail. At last and, sadly much too late, he gave his horse its head and let it try to find its own way home.

After many miles of wandering, never seeing any form of habitation, Mr. Noy was forced to dismount and lead his mount through sodden ground and thick vegitation. He had just decided that he must have left St Buryan altogether when he was overjoyed to hear music and voices. There were lights in the trees some way off, through what appeared to be an orchard. William believed that he had stumbled on some other farm where the workers were making merry at a gulthise of their own. He was surprised to notice that his dog's ears were flat to his head and his tail was between his legs. The horse seemed similarly distressed and would move no closer to the lights. William tied his mount to a tree and pushed on alone. He caught glimpses of people beyond the orchard, seated at tables, feasting and dancing together to the beat of a crowd or tambourine, played by a maiden dressed all in white. As he approached the feast he could see that the maiden was standing on the heaving stock, close by the door of a dwelling.

The revellers were in the house yard, some distance from the door. William was astonished to realise that, while the maid was of normal stature, the revellers were considerably undersized. The tables, chairs, plates, mugs and knives which they used were all in proportion with these little people. The dancers moved so swiftly that he became headlight, watching their quick and intricate, whirling movements.

William believed the maid in white to be the daughter of the master of the place for, when the dance ended, she handed to crowd to a fellow close beside her and entered the house, returning a moment later with a blackjack of liquor and went around the company dispensing it freely. When the maid retrieved the crowd and beat up a new tune for the dancers, William Noy felt that she cast a sideways glance towards him. The music was so charming and lively that he could hardly restrain himself from going to join the dancers but the girl frowned in alarm and made a motion with her head to indicate that he should go round a corner of the house, out of sight. She gave the crowd to the fellow who had guarded it previously and whispered in his ear. He immediately took up the rhythm of the dance with a will. The girl then walked into the orchard trees and signalled to William Noy to follow her.

The maid waited for William in a moonlit spot, out of sight of the merry throng at their tables. When William approached he was all but overwhelmed to see that the maid standing there before him was none other than Grace Hutchens from Selena, his sweetheart whom he believed to have died some four years since. At least, William had mourned her for dead and she had been burried as such in Buryan Churchyard.
"Thank the Lord, William" she cried, "that I managed to stop you from showing yourself or you would have been changed into the small people's state, as I am, woe is me."

William was in such a state of shock from the sight of one he had believed to be long dead that he did not take in all her words at once. He did however give way to his emotions and was about to embrace his long lost love and kiss her when she stopped him, almost violently. This surprise restored some of his wits and he was able to understand the next thing that Grace said to him.
"Oh beware!" she exclaimed "embrace me not. Touch neither flower nor fruit for eating a tempting plum in this enchanted orchard was my undoing. You may think it strange but it was through love of you that I am come to this. What was found on the moor and buried for me was some changeling or sham body, not mine. I believe this to be true for I feel now, much the same as when I lived and was your sweetheart."

"Grace, Grace! hasten and bring us more beer and cider" squeeked a little voice from the tables.
"Quick" said Grace to William, "go round behind the house and wait for me there but keep out of sight, whatever you do."
"Dear Grace, when you come, bring with you a flagon of beer or cider for I have ridden for miles tonight and am parched."
"Not for the world!" cried Grace. "Touch nothing, eat or drink nothing in this place or you will be changed as I have been and you will become servant to these sprites as I am now. Go and wait for me. I shall not be long, my love."

Grace saw to the needs of the tables and, when all were well supplied with food and drink, she sought out William and conducted him to a hidden bower, away from the merrymakers, where their noise was less troublesome. There she told him how, one evening while she was searching for some strayed sheep, she had heard William calling to his dogs. She had crossed from Selena Moor to Pendrea in the hope of meeting him when she lost her way amongst the head high bracken and soon found herself the same quagmire that had bewildered William. After wandering amongst the bogs and pools for hours, she heard the same fairy music and followed it through the orchard. Feeling weary and thirsty, she had plucked a plum which glowed like gold in the clear starlight. No sooner had she put it to her lips than it turned to bitter water in her mouth and made her sick and faint. She fell, senseless to the ground where she lay, for how long she could not tell. When at last she woke she was surrounded by the very little people whom William had seen at the feast.

The sprites seemed overjoyed to get a 'tidy girl' who would bake and brew, keep their homes and nurse their 'changed children' who weren't as sturdy as they used to be for want of beef and good malt liquor. In the years that she had performed these duties she had never come to enjoy her life amongst these small people. Everything amongst them was mere illusion or sham. They experience few of the feeling that humans do. What pleases them is merely the remembrance of what pleased them when they were mortals themselves, maybe thousands of years before. What they made to seem like ruddy apples and luscious peaches and plums were merely sloes, hips and haws. The gorgeous rare flowers which they gathered about themselves were, in reality, the common wildflowers that grow everywhere like weeds. Their food, which appeared so tempting and satisfying was but bland, washy fare which made Grace's stomach feel so waterish that she longed for a bit of salt fish. The only thing which she relished was the milk of the goats which the little people had stolen from humans. These beasts were enticed away to provide nourishment for the sprites' babes and changlings.

"And now" sighed Grace, "I am becoming used to this half life. I am treated well. The little fellow to whom I handed the crowd just now, he is particularly good to me. I told him I was going to see to the children. Oh, Willy! There is no need to look so jealous, for he is little more than vapour and love to him is no more than fancy."
"Do they have children?" asked William who had not considered such a possibility.
"Very few but when one is born amongst them there is great rejoycing. Each of the men fancies himself the father. Don't look so amazed Willy, these people are so very different from us. They are star worshippers, they do not share our beliefs. Life is so much longer amongst them that our constancy in marriage would become very tiresome. And I believe that their long life becomes a great burden to the older folk as they fade away and become almost invisible. Indeed, some of them

long for the time when they will dissolve into the air entirely and so end their wearisome existence."

"My only joy in this place is that I have been granted a gift. I can take the form of any bird I choose and, for a brief time each day, I am able to fly to be close to you. As long as you live, Willy dear, I shall rejoice to be near you and when you die, if you wish, we may be together in this fairy land. But cling to life, Willy for I would rather see you in flesh and blood than changed to my state."

Mr Noy had a heart full of questions for his Grace and was about to voice the first when he was interrupted by cries from the feast, demanding more drink, and quickly. Grace hurried from him and a hasty plan formed itself in his mind. He recalled that a turned garment would disperse such sprites as these imprisoning Grace in this place. He decided to turn the glove in his pocket inside out and pull it on to his hand before dashing into the feasting crowd to rescue his lost love.

No sooner had he begun his run towards the revellers than the lights blinked out. All the company, including Grace, disappeared in an instant. He felt a severe blow to his forehead and he became dimly aware of nothing but an old, roofless bowjy in a thorn thicket as his conciousness sliped away entirely. He lay, insensible in this place until his hound led the searchers to him and he woke to this life once more.

Those to whom Mr Noy told his tale were not surprised for similar stories had been related by others in times past. Some had mentioned that the small people were never to be seen in the daytime for they were very vain and hated to be seen in that light where they appeared so aged and grim. Others related that these folk, like Grace, were able to change their form into those of animals. At each change however they became slightly smaller and less substantial until, eventually, they became muryans or ants and were lost into the ground.

From the day when he was discovered in the bowjy on Selena Moor, Mr Noy became a changed man. He talked of little except his adventure and he fancied that every small bird that came near was his Grace, come to spend time with him. At night he would wander the Moor hoping to meet his love once more. He became melancholy and neglected both his farm and his friends. Before the next harvest time, he departed this life. Whether he truly died or passed into fairy land is not known.

Cap'n Black and Accie Carne

Now, do you remember the night when Nelly Wearne and Captain Black disappeared with the captain's bosun, Ackie Carne? My soul and body! That was some night that was. Spoken of in St Buryan to this very day it is. After the crashing thunder, the blinding lightning, the enting rain and the howling wind died away in the early morning, the people of the Church Town took stock and surveyed the damage. The church was unharmed but many other buildings had lost slates from their roofs. Their owners were considered fortunate by those who had lost their roofs entirely. One barn was utterly destroyed. A lightning strike had set the thatch alight. This barn was full of dry corn and hay and the fire had been spectacular. In the cold morning light there was little left of the structure. Everything combustible had burned and the ashes had been blown away by the tempest. When the wooden beams had been consumed, the walls had fallen in, so that the morning's visitors saw only a smoking heap of blackened stones.

A small crowd gathered in the dim daylight and some visiting merrymakers from outside the town even disputed that there had ever been a barn on the spot, the destruction was so entire. As the discussion proceeded a young boy spied something on the ground, near where the barn doors had once swung. He picked up a cloth wrapped around a sticky brown mess. The boy's mother took the cloth from her son and was about to toss it into the ruins of the barn when she saw something embroidered on the fabric. A lettered man in the assembly was asked if he knew what the stitching signified.
"N W" announced the scholar. "Those are the letters stitched here. 'Tis Nelly

Wearne's handkerchief and that mess within it is all that the rain has left of the fairings she had bought for the feast. Do they smell of ginger?"
"Ess they do my dear" said another. "And here's the silver button that burst from Nell's bodice when she was dancing. I saw she pick un up and hide un in her hankeychiff".
"And I saw the three of 'em leave the dance and enter the barn, just before that last git crash of thunder that deafened us all" said an old man on the edge of the group. "I tell ee, the Cap'n waddn none but the Old One he's self and that Ackie Carne wadn' no bosun at all, but Beelzebub out of the pit. They have taken our Nelly off and brought down fire upon she and took her down into Hell to dance for eternity."
"Dosen't ee be so daft as you are" cried the mother of the handkerchief finder. That's nothin' but foolishness."
"No ee idn' " cried a newcomer who was none but Squire Cardew's mother, she who had forbidden Nelly to go to the dance the night before. "Nelly, my dear love!" cried the dame. "I tried to keep ee home but you brought this on yerself, my golden girl, with all yer pride."
"How could you blame the poor child?" asked the scholar.
"Because" wailed the dame, "as she stormed out of my kitchen she boasted that she would dance at feast, even if it was with the Devil he's self. That's why!"

Squire said it was all nonsense. He thought Nelly had simply gone off with a sailor from some boat and would be back before too long, a little wiser for her adventures. Squire was wrong, for Nelly was never seen again by him or by any of his kin. Like many landowners of his time, Squire Cardew was fonder of hunting and drinking than he was of farming. He became fonder still of these pastimes after his Nelly was taken from him and, consequently, his fortune slowly faded. Eventually, he found himself reduced to the position of servant to the gentleman to whom he was forced to sell all his lands and goods. Madam Cardew died of a broken heart long before the Squire's fall from fortune. Nelly was her joy, in spite of the girl's wayward ways. Without Nelly's singing and dancing to gladden the lot of the old lady, the life went out of her and she was soon laid to rest.

So, had Nelly and Captain Black plunged into Hades with Ackie Carne? Quite the opposite. Squire Cardew was right. The Captain did take Nelly onto his ship and sailed off with her in search of adventure and fortune. Nelly took to men's attire on board ship but this didn't prevent her from producing a son and heir for Cap'n Black. Just before the boy was born the two married so that the child could take the Captain's name. This regularising of their situation had no further effect because the Cap'n and crew took to a life of piracy and smuggling and soon amassed a fortune in gold, silver and jewels. Further fortunes were won, lost, regained, buried and lost again while the pirate family grew and flourished.

Eventually, the Cap'n started to tire of the buccaneering life and Nelly began hankering after her home and family and the ship, the 'Lovely Nell', soon found herself in Cornish waters once more. Nelly was landed near St Buryan and was

promised that she would be collected from Mousehole whenever she sent word to the 'Lovely Nell'. To natives, Nell looked entirely foreign as she moved from farm to farm, asking after the Cardews of Boskenna. No one took her for a returning native but believed her to be a wandering gypsy. But no gypsy was as richly attired as Nelly Wearne in her brocades and her black hair wound round her head and covered with the scarlethood of her mantel. The Cardews were remembered but it seemed that all were now dead. The old squire who had sold the last of the property and stayed on to serve the new owner had only recently been buried. Nell believed herself to be the last member of her family remaining alive when she called at the cottage of Betty Trenoweth. Yes, the same Betty as she who cussed Madam Noy and her coppies.

She knocked on Betty's door and when the old woman answered she asked "Don't you recognise me, Betty?"
"I don't believe I do, my dear. I don't believe I've had the pleasure." But when she looked into those dark eyes she saw a familiar light dancing there and she cried "Oh my blessed Lord I do believe it's Nelly Wearne." And the two women fell into each other's arms, laughing and crying at the same time. It had been twenty years since the two had seen each other and the rest of the day, and most of the following night, was spent painting in the blank portions of their histories. Betty had many a tale to tell about the exercise of her powers over her gullible neighbours. Eventually, Nelly began to tell Betty the truth about what had happened at Buryan Feast, all those years ago. It was less fantastic but more exciting than any stories of black magic or witchcraft that had been rumoured about the lost maid.

Billy Bray, to use Cap'n Black's original name, was a poor, distant relation from Pendeen who often visited the Cardews when Nelly was a young girl. The two young people became, at first, fond of each other and eventually, deeply in love. When Billy had grown to full manhood and was about to ask Squire Cardew for Nelly's hand, ill fortune befell him. He was challenged to fight by another Pendeen man and had, unintentionally, killed his opponent in the ensuing battle. Forced into hiding, Billy had continued to meet secretly with Nelly and the pair had hatched the elaborate plan to elope on the night of Buryan Feast. Both knew that the Squire would never allow a murderer to enter into his family. Nelly and Billy, or Cap'n Black, had run away together to live a life of adventure and free trading on the high seas. The faithful Accie Carne had accompanied the pair and the three adventurers, having amassed a considerable fortune, had returned to spend the autumn of their years in the homeland they loved so much. They had more than enough riches to buy a farm and live a life of peace and plenty near Tresidder. Nelly might have lived happily for ever more but the Cap'n couldn't settle down to what he called a land lubber's lazy life. After a few years he and the bosun, who had been with him all this time, took to the high seas and lived the life of adventure once more. As soon as Nelly's son was old enough to accompany his father on these voyages, Nelly found herself all alone on the Tresidder Farm. The 'Lovely Nell' returned regularly to Cornish waters but, after each romantic lovers' reunion, his wander lust soon drove Cap'n Black back to sea.

After one particularly successful smuggling trip, Cap'n Black and his crew were returning home and battling against a storm of such intensity of thunder and lightning that the crew feared for their lives. The Cap'n, sensing their fear cried out "Hoist away all sail boys for, by the Devil, we'll get home tonight." The boat flew before the wind like a living thing. The crew fully expected to be wrecked for, at every flash of lightning, the granite cliffs were seen to be a little closer. The accompanying fusillade of thunder hammered home the message of imminent doom. Cap'n Black, making fun of his crew's fears cried out "Bravo, you devils of the whirlwind, fire away and we will salute you with our own thunder." Giving the helm to Ackie Carne, he loaded and fired the swivel gun in answer to the cannonade from the skies.
"There, fellow devils" cried the Cap'n, "take that. Stand by me now and I'll be with 'ee soon."
The following sheet of lightning burst over the sea, the cliffs, rocks and carns, illuminating them as plainly as if it were day. The sheet of flame hung across the cove mouth long enough to allow the Lovely Nell to slip safely in and almost immediately, the storm died away.

With the goods safely landed, the smugglers lit a fire on the beach and opened a few barrels of good liquor to celebrate their safe return. As the men relaxed after their ordeal, Cap'n Black drew the keg on which he sat, a little closer to the fire. The keg was not a sound one and one of its seams opened under the burden of the Cap'n's weight. All at once his breath seemed to be ablaze and his body surrounded by flames. Ackie Carne was first to notice the calamity and flung himself into the living brand to save his Cap'n. The two overbalanced and fell, bursting the barrel and allowing the spirit to escape and explode with such violence that no trace of either of the two men was found when the horrified crew surveyed the scene in the next morning's light. 'As you sow, so shall you reap' as the Bible de say.

And what became of Nelly? She sold her farm at Tresidder and went to live with Betty Trenoweth. Betty was living the life of a recluse in her little cottage on the outskirts of St Buryan. Her reputation as a wise woman had grown over the years but the suspicion that she was also a witch gave her respect amongst the community but precious little company. Betty welcomed Nelly into her home and the two women renewed their friendship which had begun when Nelly was still only a girl at Boskenna.

"Tis as good as a play, my dear" said Betty, "to see the old women of Church town trying to find out who you are. And they can't discover for I take good care to fool them. They are mad to know why you keep indoors except for your early morning walk down to the cliffs or your moonlight excursions."
"And what did you tell them then, An Betty?" asked Nelly.
"I told the curious, prying fools that you are a wise woman come from the East and that you venture out to gather herbs at particular times of day and night. I said that you are particularly skilled at making salves and potions and that you can cure anything from the gripes to the palsy. Now all the wenches want to know if you can read fortunes because they believe you to be a gypsy. I've told them that you can read hands and can tell who will be married and who will not. They now believe that you know more about white witchcraft than the Witch of Endor who we hear so much about."
"But I know nothing of such things, Betty" cried Nelly, alarmed at what her friend had been claiming on her behalf.
"Matter do uh if you don't?" answered Betty with a wink. "What you do know is the history of every family hereabouts up to twenty year ago and I can tell ee what's happened since. When they find you know their past they will easily believe you can tell their future."
"I can try, but how will I know who is who when they come?" asked Nell.
"Keep to the parlour and I shall come and see you before I bring them in" answered Betty. "When they come in to ee, be sure to hint at some scandal that happened to their family, no matter how long ago. Then you can promise them any number of sweethearts and a speedy marriage. Just say what you wished for yourself as a young girl."

All worked well at first but a change of plan was needed when older, plain spinsters heard about Nellie's powers and came seeking hope for themselves. To these, Nellie gave less plain answers and coupled these with advice on how best to snare what few men of their own age and older who remained single and available. Some were supplied with love powders and others with compounds to freshen a husband's interest in his wife.

Little more is known for sure about Nelly Wearne. The last hint of her existence appears in the account of a school in St Buryan, more than two hundred years ago. This document contains a description of the school Dame, a handsome, dark woman who wore outlandish garments. The good dame was reported to entertain her charges, when they had worked well at their lessons, with tales of her buccaneering relatives and their daring exploits at sea, many years before.

Cap'n Trahare's Voyages

Cap'n Trahare was born in the cove. He wasn't Cap'n Trahare then of course, just plain Billy. His Da was lost at sea before Billy could speak so his Ma raised the boy on her own without realising just *how* 'on her own' she would become. Before Billy was two, the mine failed and the neighbours left for the village up the valley. They soon forgot the cove, Billy and Billy's Ma. The deserted cottages slowly dissolved back into the ground from which they had been built and when Billy was five, only Inez Trahare's home and a few heaps of stones remained.

Inez did her best to educate the boy. By the age of ten, Billy could read a little but he couldn't write at all. Inez worked her garden and Billy fished from the rocks enclosing the sandy cove. They fed their stove with drift wood and made candles from any tallow which floated ashore. Inez was content in her isolation but Billy craved other company. He would push through the furze and bramble choking the path, up to the village to sell spare fish or garden produce. This brought in enough cash to buy those items the cove could not supply.

Cap'n Trahare's Voyages

The village children bullyragged the boy whenever he appeared. Many of the adults were as cruel as their offspring, taking delight in cheating Billy when he offered to trade fish and produce for other necessities. Johnny Cox, who had fished with Billy's Da, was the only villager to treat the boy kindly. Johnny, now a farm worker, no longer needed his fishing cap and gave it to Billy, together with a new name, 'Cap'n Trahare'. Thrilled with his cap and title, Billy rushed home.
"I'm a Cap'n now Ma. I got a hat to prove it. I ought to have a boat."
"There's plenty craft down beach, Billy Booy. Been there for years but they're only fit for fire wood. Never mind my 'ansome. Come here to yer Ma and I'll read ee a story from yer faither's books."

Billy's Father had been a great reader. The boy loved to hear tales from Da's books whenever his Ma could spare the time. Billy would follow the words as best he could and daydream about the yarns he heard. At night, Billy dreamed new stories, more fantastic even than those in the books. Now, with his captain's cap and title, he dreamed of adventures aboard his own ship. The boy decided to investigate the abandoned boats.

Most of the craft lay in damp sand and their bottoms had rotted away. One punt, however, was upended on some rocks where the wind kept it relatively dry so its timbers were still sound. Thrilled at this discovery, Billy dragged the little boat to a deep pool and pushed it in. Slowly, it filled and sank, along with Billy's hopes. He told his Ma what had happened.
"Gosson booy! Ee de prob'ly need nothin' more'n caulking up and a lick of tar to keep un water tight. I'll find ee some old stuff to shred up and shove into the joints to make un tight and tidy. Got any oars 'av ee?"
"One come ashore last winter, Ma" said Billy "but haven't ee got to have two?"
"One'll do for now booy. Leave us get the boat a bit fitty and I shall show ee 'ow to scull. You de only need one oar for that. By-'n-by you might be lucky and find another. Then I shall tell ee 'ow to go 'bout rowin' proper job. Find a spar or two and a bit of canvas and thes'll be sailin' soon."

Billy climbed the valley to share news of his boating progress and details of his dreams with Johnny Cox. Johnny would listen but all the others laughed at his efforts. Hurt, Cap'n Trahare learned to keep himself, his tales and his dreams, to himself. His journeys up the valley became few and far between.

Then, Billy's mother died, leaving the boy alone. He climbed the valley for help and a funeral was arranged. The men pushed through the furze and bramble with an empty coffin and then stumbled back, up hill, with a full one. No one from the village ever felt inspired to repeat the journey. Cap'n Trahare was left alone with his dreams and his imagination to make what sense he could of the world.

Billy began each day walking the tide line, looking for treasure; shells, rope, seaweed, bottles and wood. After gathering these 'mermaids' gifts', the Cap'n would tend his garden. When the weeds were tamed he would scull out to check his lines and pots and collect his catch. If there was anything spare, he might climb the valley to trade.

After each busy day, the Cap'n slept soundly while the night crammed his head with dreams. Often, he dreamed of a silver strand set in a sapphire sea. Brilliant birds sang sweet songs in the forests fringing the beach. At first he wandered this wide waste of sand, content with the wonders he found there but, one night, his curiosity led him into the trees behind the beach. Just as the dreaming beach was wider and more wonderful than his day time cove, the forest made his waking woods of scratching bramble and prickling furze inconsequential. These trees were so full of fruit that their boughs bowed down, proffering their bounty to the Cap'n as he passed. There was a heavy, heady, scent of flowers which, together with the brilliant birds, splashed the forest with vivid colour.

One night, emboldened by his discoveries, the Cap'n ventured beyond the forest and came upon a city, filled with dreamers like himself. Their kingly leader welcomed him into their forum and bade him sit and enjoy the entertainment. The tales he heard that night delighted the Cap'n but his joy increased tenfold when his own stories, so scorned in the village, were warmly welcomed here. On each succeeding night, after beaching his vessel, the Cap'n would hurry through the forest and into the forum to trade tales. One night there was greater excitement than usual. The Old King had served his term. A new leader must be found before morning. Whoever told the most fantastic tale that night would rule as King in the city for the coming year.

Each teller told a tale, more wondrous than the last, and when the Cap'n's turn came, he dug deep amongst his dreams for a fable to conquer all that had gone before. He wove a wondrous web from fragments from his father's books and memories of his lonely life. The Cap'n's tale complete, there was no sound, applause or cry of praise. The crown was simply lifted up and placed upon his head.

That morning, as on every other, Cap'n Trahare woke to disappointment at finding himself once more in his cove. A walk along the strand to find his 'mermaid gifts' would raise his spirits a little but the discontent lingered long, even seeping into his other, dreaming life. On one night the Cap'n, feeling himself to be an unworthy companion for his subjects, wandered away from the forum and into a nearby scented garden. Instead of the seclusion he sought there, he found a group of maidens, fair beyond his imaginings, dancing in a grove. For forty nights the Cap'n neglected his friends and wooed the leader of this troupe until the kingdom could rejoice to hear that they would have a Queen.

How the Cap'n longed to leave his waking cove where each day dawned to disappointment. But the mighty ocean waves always seemed too great for his tiny craft. Slowly, resolution grew within him. He thought to himself; 'the boat I beach on the enchanted shore each night is the same boat that dances on the waves, there in the cove. If my waking boat is also the boat of my dreams then it will steer itself to the *place* of my dreams. I shall set sail now, this very afternoon.' And with that, he set off on his voyage.

The swell beyond the protecting arms of his cove was mighty and the Cap'n found himself in a deep watery pit one minute and then gazing from a marine mountain peak the next. Each time he spied the land it seemed a little further off it and, eventually, it disappeared completely. The sun sank and a strong breeze sprang up and drove the little boat before it. The unaccustomed motion soon made the Cap'n ill and he spent many long hours in this sorry state until, finally, sleep overcame his misery and granted him a little peace.

When he awoke he found that he had been driven into a wide, sandy bay. The Cap'n's heart lept within him. Was this not the land of his dreams? Beyond the sand he should find the forest of birds and the orchard of exotic fruit. Turning his back on the sea, the Cap'n set off in search of breakfast. Soon the sound of the sea had faded and the air filled with bird song. In his dream the forest of fruit was close to the shore but here there were no trees and the birds, for all their sweet song were drab brown, not brightly coloured as he had expected. He climbed a low hedge and there, spread before him, was the fruit he sought, laid upon the ground or hanging from low bushes. And so many sorts! And growing in such regular rows! There were even baskets in which to collect the fruit and so . . . collect it he did. He ate enough to satisfy his hunger and then filled a basket to enjoy later, while he explored his new land. Blackberries, bitter elderberries and sour sloes were the only fruit the Cap'n had enjoyed before. Here was such vast variety of new and tantalising tastes. Some were softly sweet while other treats were tart but tasty.

The shout which came from the far side of the field was no subject's salute. There was anger and threat in the cry, signaling the approach of a short, stout woman. She made the mistake of waving the stick which she usually relied upon for support. This slowed her progress sufficiently to allow the Cap'n an easy escape. Beyond the field lay a broad road along which he ran until he came to a small wood where he rested, deciding what to do next. He must take greater care! There could be other differences between this place and his dream kingdom. He lay low in the wood until evening and then followed the road once more and soon entered a city by the sea. The streets were filled with friendly folk, some dressed in outlandish costumes and all moving in concert towards the harbour. Cap'n Trahare was greeted by a group of revelers who welcomed him into their company. They asked him who he was and what plans he had for Midsummer Eve. The Cap'n told of his dreams and how he intended to make them come true. And now, in his *waking* life, the Cap'n's tales were applauded. He was made to feel an equal amongst his companions who told him he should become mayor of this merry seaside place. But first he must be selected by the whole community, waiting in a pavilion nearby to choose their leader.

One by one, rival claimants were thrust forth to proclaime their qualifications for the mighty office. The Cap'n was awed by their eloquence and shocked at the shouts and jeers of the electorate. Fearing that his poor attempts would be greeted with even more derision, he would have withdrawn from the contest but his friends pushed him forward when he was called. Every word he spoke was loudly applauded by his company. His companions' praise was infectious and soon the whole audience was cheering the Cap'n and demanding he be made Mayor. A great chain of office was hung around his neck. He was hoisted high and paraded through the streets led by a mighty band of musicians. The crowd danced a sinuous, serpantine dance throughout the town in celebrations which lasted for many hours until, exhausted, the new Mayor was taken to a small, stone built palace, facing the sea with convenient couches upon which he was invited to take his ease. The Cap'n slept soundly until the sun blazed in midsummer glory from behind a great castle on an island across the bay.

He looked around but the broad seaside path, so full of life the night before, was deserted so the New Mayor made his way back to the town place. Early as it was, his subjects were already decorating his realm with green boughs and setting up booths for a great market. Each wore a spray of yellow flowers and soon Cap'n Trahare had one too. The revelers greeted him and begged him too walk in state at the head of gay processions which threaded their way through the streets. Wonderful entertainments were offered, right there in the street, by jugglers, acrobats, singers and dancers.

Oh the dancers! They were just as beautiful and enticing as the dancers in his dream. All he needed to fulfill his destiny was to choose one of these sirens for his Queen or was it Mayoress? And there she was, in the middle of the dance, swaying to the music, smiling at the Cap'n and telling him, with her eyes that it was she who was destined to be the Cap'n's consort.

Emboldened, Cap'n Trahare stepped into the dance and up to his chosen bride. The music faltered and stopped as the Cap'n told his beloved;
"I have chosen you, the fairest of all fair maidens, to be my Mayoress and I shall lead you out from this dance and make you the mother of my children". A great hush fell. The crowd became restless and fell back as a giant of a man stepped forward and joined the Cap'n and his dancer in the ring. His voice was even louder than the voice of that forgotten crone in the field of fruit.
"No you bleady aren't, my 'ansome!" said the giant and the sun glinted off his shaven head and off the great muscles on his arms "or I shall 'ave somethin' to say about it."
This hadn't happened in the Cap'n's dream. Come to think of it, there was no angry, stick waving woman in his dream forest of fruit either. He realized that he couldn't rely too heavily on dream detail. The giant spoke again.
"Shall us put up with this booys? He seem to b'lieve that, just because we made un Mock Mayor he can do what he like and make he's self a nuisance to our maidens."

'Mock Mayor!' That was a shock. There was no 'Mock' in his dream and shouldn't he be King and not just 'Mayor'?
Once more the great voice boomed.
"You can put up with un if you de like but I aren't goin to be hinsulted by no skinny little rabbit of a mad man with his daft yarns that might be good enough for Mazy Eve but don't make no sense at all in broad daylight. Make he's self a nuisance to my Zelda would uh?" he shouted to the crowd. "Not if I got anythin' to do with it ee wain't!" and he looked round for the Cap'n and then cried in amazement "Wheresato?"

And well might he have cried, for the Cap'n was no fool. He had melted into the crowd and had begun to run as soon as all attention was focused on the giant.. Off up hill he ran; the giant and the crowd roaring behind him. Even after leaving the town he could still hear them baying in the distance. Eventually he reached moorland, filled with wind and where there was no other sound. There were no houses and, more importantly, no people in this desolation. Gradually he began to feel secure once more and lay down to rest.

What was that? It could have been a cow lowing but Billy started up once more, convinced the giant was still chasing. On and on he rushed. Each time he slackened his pace, some other imagined alarm set him off again until, exhausted, he found himself running downhill. He gathered speed and tripped, and fell. Down and down the steep slope he rolled. The slope became steeper and steeper. Billy rolled faster and faster until he could no longer tell which way was up and which was not. Each rock he bounced off knocked more breath from his battered body. Finally he came to a halt in a prickle of furze and bramble.

As his senses returned he noticed the slight traces of a path which seemed familiar. The sun was sinking as he pushed down, through the gorse towards his cove. There was a good crop of mermaids' gifts on the tide line. He would wait until morning to collect these. First he would lie on his little bed in the lonely cottage and sink into a thankful sleep, sail his boat and swap stories with his friends and be content at last to dream his dreams.

Trouble at Treen

It was the evening of 8th April 1824 and the bar parlour of the Ship Inn at Mousehole was busy as usual. There was a rather subdued merriment such as you might find at the inn of any poor fishing village where the maximum enjoyment had to be extracted from the small amount of spare cash to be found in a fisherman's pocket. Nevertheless, the clamour was sufficient to spoil the temper of the young naval officer billeted at the inn. Lieutenant Hugh Goldsmith was master of the revenue cutter, Nimble. His was the task of ensuring that no brandy, tobacco, silk, tea, lace or other luxury goods were landed in this part of Cornwall without the payment of duty which had been stipulated by His Majesty's Government.

Lt. Goldsmith knew that the occupants of the Ship Inn parlour were 'free traders' and the occupants of the parlour knew that he knew. In case you aren't familiar with the term, a free trader is one who feels that trade should be free of all restraints, especially the curse of having to pay King George's duty on their goods. You might know these business men better by the more vulgar term of 'smugglers'. Fishermen could not avoid starvation when the fishing was poor if they did not have other ways of earning a crust for their families. The main means of providing for a family when there were no fish, was free trading. You might think, as they did, that the needs of their wives and children were much more important than the needs of King George IV, who always seemed to have enough to eat and, as far as they knew, never had to go fishing.

The free trading gentlemen had their little boats and could meet vessels from France or Holland, out at sea, away from the prying eyes of the revenue men. There they could take aboard goods at prices much lower than they would fetch in an English town. There were plenty of citizens willing to buy these goods at a fair price and many places to hide the merchandise around the rocky coast with its hidden coves and caves. The revenue men were a nuisance but there were ways and means of avoiding trouble from them as you will hear shortly.

Trouble at Treen

Lt. Goldsmith called for the landlord but it was his wife who answered the summons.
"Your dinner won't be a moment, Lt. Goldsmith" said Nancy Roseworthy. "I've got you a fine piece of beef tonight, sir."
"I'm sure the beef will be excellent but can you do something about that damned row in the bar" said her guest. "I'm sure they make that racket simply to annoy me. Just because I'm putting a stop to their damned games and making them do an honest day's work instead of cheating His Majesty out of his revenues. Tell them to be silent, will you."
"I'm afraid I can't do that, sir" said Nancy, apologetically. "The men won't be silenced. They come in for a little entertainment and, Lord knows, they get little enough of it for their lives are very hard."
"Hard! They don't know the meaning of the word" cried Lt. Goldsmith. "And if you can't silence the dogs then send your husband in to do the job for you."

Mrs Roseworthy rushed from the room. She was a rather timid woman to be the landlady of an inn and left most of the dealings with customers to her husband who possessed a much stronger character. The good lady had welcomed the idea of having a navel officer to lodge at the inn for she believed that he would raise the tone of the place by his presence. The surly Lieutenant was not what she had expected at all and she was rather in awe of him. She rushed to tell her husband about the Lieutenant's complaint but was dismayed when he was far from sympathetic to his guest's demands.
"Don't worry yourself, Nancy" he told his wife. "Get him some beef and gravy quickly and I'll see to his complaints. He has an infernal cheek, expecting silence when the place turns into a mad house every time his damned sailors come through the door."
"Oh! I do worry, Charley" cried his wife. "We need more people, the likes of he, if we're goin' to raise the class of this place but I aren't no good at doin' with 'em."

"I can deal with the lieutanant, Nancy, my love. And as to the class of the place, well, face it my dear, it's an inn in a fishing village. How we goin' to do much about that?"
Oh, Charlie!" his wife complained, "all the other ladies up to Paul church of a Sunday, I'm sure they de look down on we with our little inn and our shabby things."
"I don't want to hear nothin' about they, Nancy. "We're as good as any of 'em and a damned sight more honest than most up there, for all their goin' to church on a Sunday mornin' and then cheatin' their neighbours the rest of the week. Now, off you go and get the lieutenant his dinner my dear. I'll see to his complaints."

Nancy returned to the kitchen to hurry the dinner along while Charlie Roseworthy strode into the small, best dining room which the officer had to himself.
"Its good to see you back here so soon, Lt. Goldsmith" announced the landlord jovially. "Nancy tells me your dinner won't be a minute. I have a sturdy piece of beef for you tonight, sir. Would you like a bottle of wine to go with it or perhaps you would prefer ale from the bar?"
"Damn your ale, landlord. Have you any of that fine wine you gave me last trip?"
"I always keep a few bottles of good wine for special guests, sir" the landlord told him. "I'll fetch it from the cellar myself. Ah! Here's Alice with your dinner. Set it down on the table, girl and fetch a glass while I get the wine"

The lieutenant had begun his meal when the landlord returned with a very dusty bottle and a corkscrew. Charlie Roseworthy began to pour out the wine.
"I hope this is none of that damned, smuggled brew that you're serving me, Landlord" said the Lieutenant.
"See for yourself, sir" said the landlord, showing his guest the bottle. "It's from a very respectable wine merchant in Truro, sir. The self same as is patronised by the Lord Lieutenant of the County himself. Just look there, at the label, sir. Why, I wouldn't take the risk of losing my licence to save a few pence on any witches brew that might be smuggled in. I have my reputation to think of, sir. I'm well known for keeping the best wines in the west of the county."
"Glad to hear it, landlord." said his guest. "It wouldn't do for me to be found drinking smuggled liquor in my position."
"No indeed Lt. Goldsmith" replied the landlord. "I know that it does go on around here, smuggling and worse, but I'm known for an honest inn keeper sir, and no free trader has had the brass neck to offer me his trash for he'd know what to expect."
"I'm glad to hear it" said his guest "but you must hear hints about smuggling in a small place like this. If you could tip me the wink when something's afoot then it could be very much to your advantage."
"I should be honoured to help His Majesty's officers in their duty" said Charlie Roseworthy, keeping his fingers crossed in his pocket. "The free traders spoil the trade for us honest men. I should be glad to see some of them get their just deserts, sir."
"Good man. My superiors in Plymouth don't know what I'm up against down here. I have to catch the villains red handed or it's impossible to get a conviction. Even then the few who will testify in court only support the cock and bull stories that the devils concoct."
"I can see that such things must be a grave trial to your honour" said the landlord.
"Grave isn't the word for it man" agreed Lt. Goldsmith. "Now, tell me. What does a gentleman do for sport in this place?
"There's not a lot of game these days sir, mostly the gentry has to make do with rabbits and hares" said the landlord.
"Damn me, man!" cried the Lieutenant. "I need something more entertaining than a few conies. Are there no other diversions at all? What about this logging

rock I hear about. Is that nearby?"
"The logging rock at Treen? Oh, that's a wonder, that is. You must see that, sir" said the landlord.
"It says in the book by this fellow Borlaise, that no human power can overthrow the stone, though it may be rocked by a child."
"That's right, sir" the landlord assured him. "I've rocked it myself. It must weigh a hundred tons, and yet a touch can set it moving just like a rocking chair."
This news seemed to impress the lieutenant. "Hmm. Yes, well, I suppose I must pay it a visit. A hundred tons, you say? That's quite a weight. Has anyone tried to knock it over?"
"Not to my knowledge, sir" answered the landlord. "Why on earth would anyone want to try?"
"Why indeed, landlord?" said the lieutenant absently. "Now, man, send some of your excellent brandy up to my room and tell the girl to call me at six in the morning. We're sailing early tomorrow."
"Very well sir" said his host. "And a good night to you, Lieutenant Goldsmith."

Between the cliff castle at Treen and the Minack Rock there is a wide stretch of golden shingle which is mostly enclosed by steep granite cliffs. On the morning following Lt. Goldsmith's learning about the Logan Rock, the Richards brothers from Penberth Cove were working in the surf. The tide was low as Dick and Reuben were busy moving a large collection of wooden kegs up the beach to a cave at the foot of the cliff. Their young nephew Saul was helping out generally while his father, Jacca Richards kept watch. A small French fishing boat was disappearing south-eastwards, towards the horizon.

The winter had been a hard one. The fishing had been poor and this consignment of rum and brandy was important to the Richards family's survival. As the brothers worked, Reuben was rehearsing his favourite grudge against the Harvey family who farmed at Treen and against George Harvey in particular. George was landlord of the Treen Inn.
"If we had some kin in Pezance, Dick Booy, It wouldn't be so bad" complained Reuben.
"What wouldn't be so bad?" asked his brother.
"They Harveys from Treen are getting all the trade, showing folks round the Logan Rock and we don't get none of it" answered Reuben. "As soon as the visitors arrive at Penzance, they Harveys is waiting for 'em. There's Harveys workin' in the Inns at Penzance who de fix up all the trips to the rock before we has a chance. Try as we might, we only gets a couple of odd ones to show round all week an' they Harveys get upset when we gets even they crumbs!"
"Well, matter do uh?" said Dick. "We got the fishin' and this trade to keep to keep us goin'. We shain't starve, booy."
"Us might, Dick my 'ansome" warned Reuben. "They revenue cutters are sniffing round these waters more and more. It's gettin' some hard to make a honest

living with 'em around all the time. A bit of trade from the visitors would help out a lot, if they Harveys hadn't squeezed us out like they have, Damn their eyes."

There was a lull in the conversation while the brothers continued working with their latest consignment of goods from France. Reuben was still thinking about the Harvey problem when Dick gave a cry.
"What ee want Dick boy?"
"Its Jacca" replied Dick, "ees waving."
"Must be something wrong" said Reuben. "Send the boy to see what ee is."
"Saul! Saul!" cried Dick. "Run over to the point and see what yer Da de want."
"Right you are, Uncle Dick" shouted the young lad who turned and sped off along the water's edge towards the point where his father was watching. Reuben assessed the possible causes of Jacca's alarm.
"Commest on, Dick, We might have to hide this lot so lets get un together and ready to move."
"But we got to shift un tonight Reuben" said Dick. "I got deliveries to make. I've 'ad to work 'ard and long to find folks willing to risk buying from we. The Revenue de creep round the Inns as well as make theirselves a nuisance to we, you knaw. Other folks can end up in Bodmin goal and I don't want to give them no excuse to stop buyin' from us."
"Hold yer tongue Dick, Here's Saul commin' back. What do Jacca want boy?"
"Ee says it's the Nimble," panted the boy, "sailing close to the shore so ees only just seen 'er. She'll be round the point in a quarter of an hour, Reuben."
Dick looked in dismay at the collection of kegs on the sand. "We can't shift this lot back in the cave in that time. We shall have to leave un ere and run for it."
"Well! You forgot your customers some soon, Dick Richards!" said Reuben contemptuously. "Stay where you are, the pair of ee. I aren't losing this lot. I'm the one who's paid all that money to they Frenchies, not you. Saul, boy, fast as you can. Back in the cave and get they spades. Move boy!"
Dick was appalled. "Spades! We can't fight against marines with spades"

Reuben's cool head in a crisis was what made him leader of the free trading Richards family, in spite of his being Dick's junior by some seven years. "We got fifteen minutes te bury this Dick, out where the tide is floodin' so that the disturbance will be washed away while we're hidin' in the rocks. We can sail the Kitty round when the water's come up a bit and dig un out again. That's a good boy Saul" he said to the lad who had returned with a load of spades. "Now go an' fetch Jacca back here te help with the digging. What ee waitin' for Dick lad? Start shiftin' that sand. Just deep enough for the kegs mind. We haven't no time for digging no graves today booy."

Lt. Goldsmith and the First Mate of the Revenue Cutter, Nimble arrived at the foot of the crag on which the Logan Rock logged.
"That's the beggar up there is it? Well, no point standing here, Mr James. Up we

go" said the officer as he started on the last stage of the ascent. "Come on man. They tell me that ancient old ladies can climb up here. Up with you!"

The two men soon reached the top and Lt. Goldsmith was the first to set the rock logging.
"Well, well! Mr. James. The stories were true, It is as easy to rock as a cradle and it must weigh at least the hundred tons they claim. Have a try for yourself."
The Mate tried his turn and was as surprised as his Lieutenant at the ease with which the boulder responded to his touch. Impressed as he had been at first, Lt. Goldsmith soon tired of the game and tried rocking the stone more and more violently. Try as he might, the rock kept in its socket in the crag.
"Borlaise wrote that no human power could overthrow the stone" mused Lt. Goldsmith. "he hadn't reckoned on the might of the British Navy. Run down to the longboat, Mr James, and tell the crew to go back to the Nimble, fetch some hand spikes and get back up here at the double."

The sea had risen enough for the Richards' boat, the Kitty, to run into the bay and anchor above where the kegs had been buried earlier. There was less than six feet of water beneath her keel so it would be a simple job to put a man or two over the side to pull the barrels out of the sand and heave them over the gunwale.
"But we cain't lift the cargo while the Nimble's anchored only half a mile away, Reuben" complained Dick.
"Dick boy, I tell you that ship's deserted" Reuben reassured his brother. "All we got to do is pretend to be fishin' and put Jacca over the side an' lift the kegs out."
"Look, Uncle Reuben." shouted Saul who was set on watch. "All of the soldiers are up on the Logan Rock. They'll see us for sure."
"What do it matter if they do, boy" said Reuben. "We're fishermen aren't we, and the Kitty's a fishing boat, id'n she? The best thing for we te do is te drop a few lines over the side."
"Dossen ee be so daft, Reuben!" was Dick's worried response to this suggestion. "Any fool de know you wain't catch nothing here at this state of the tide. They'll never believe we're fishing."
"Any fool but a Revenue man" Reuben told him. "What do they know about fishing? They have to employ reg'lar seamen to sail the Nimble for em *and* they pays them a pittance. Play the game and they wain't be no wiser. We'll keep the Kitty between they and Jacca, and they shan't see un. Besides they de seem to be very interested in somethin' under the rock. Not one of they has so much as looked this way since I been watchin'."
"It's all very well for you to take such a risk for the rest of us!" moaned Dick.
"I aren't movin' from this point until them kegs is aboard, Dick" insisted Reuben. "The only thing that's going to get the attention of the crew of the Nimble is some damn fool like you goin' over the side and swimming for shore."
"You knaw damm well I cain't swim Reuben Richards" said Dick.

"Well shut yer mouth and stow the kegs when Jacca drags them out of the sand" Reuben ordered. "Saul an me'll work the lines on t'other side to draw attention away from ee. There now, tide's dropped enough. Over you goes Jacca booy.

"Heave!" cried Horace James, first mate aboard The Nimble. The men heaved as best they could, standing in the little space available on top of the crag.
"It gets stuck in that same place every time, Mr James" said Lt Goldsmith. Put your backs into it, you dogs. I want to see more effort."
The men have been workin' for half an hour, non-stop, sir" said The Mate. "I don't think they've got much strength left. And, sir, begging your pardon, do you think we should be throwing the rock over at all, sir?"
"Don't be such a woman, Mr. James. The rock's presence is an affront to the power of the Navy, man. It's our duty to throw it over now, to prove the power of His Majesty's seamen."
"Well, sir, in that case perhaps we could try just one man rocking and the others standing ready with their hand spikes to put their utmost strength behind the rock when it is at the extreme of its swing."
"I see what you mean Mr. James" agreed the Lieutenant. "Right, lads. Get round the other side. Do as Mr James says. And Mr James, you do the rocking and that'll be one more with the hand spikes. Rock away, Mr James. Right, lads? Wait, wait, wait, now, heave!"

It took another five minutes of work to find the exact, right moment for the men to apply their combined force and make the rock continue it's movement and not return to it's point of balance. There was a grating sound as the rock moved from its socket and began sliding down the crag. The grating built to a roar as earth and other small boulders were dragged down by the dethroned stone. There was a shuddering thud as the main mass hit the ground beneath the crag and then silence save for the cry of a lone seagull, hanging on the wind above the scene.

It was Lt. Goldsmith who broke the silence.
"Well, well, well! Beyond the power of men, eh!" he said a little nervously.
"You've done it now, Sir" observed Mr James with an ambiguous note in his voice which annoyed his Lieutenant.
"Yes, *we've* done it" said Lt. Goldsmith hoping to spread the responsibility for the achievement a little.
"Perhaps we should return to the boat, sir" suggested the mate. The locals are likely to hear about this soon and they may be upset to hear of the fall of the rock."
"And why on earth should they be upset?" asked Lt. Goldsmith.
"I believe" replied the Mate "that some of them make their living by conducting visitors around the Rock and if it don't log no more then there goes their livelihood, sir."

"Perhaps you're right, Mr James. It don't do to upset the natives even if they are likely to be the very smugglers we're here to apprehend. And anyway its getting late and we don't want to be climbing down these cliffs in the dark do we. You carry on. Mr James."
"Aye, aye, Sir. Alright you men, pick up those handspikes, the party's over. Back to the boats, boys."

"If you cain't be quiet, go and make yer infernal noise outside!" roared Charlie Roseworthy. "There's men here who want to know what's afoot in the world so give 'em the courtesy of a bit of peace and quiet or I shall chuck ee all out in the rain and you can go home and have yer old women shoutin' at ee. And from what I've heard they de roar a sight louder than me, most of 'em."

The uproar in the bar parlour died away at the landlord's outburst. Charlie was known to carry out his threats and no one wanted to be thrown out of the pub. The politicians of the Ship Inn crowded round their landlord who was also their window onto the doings in the world. There was little call for reading spectacles in Mousehole for all that the sight here was no better than in any other town.
"Now, where was I to"? asked Charlie. "Ah yes! The bit about the Logan Rock up to Treen."
Pausing for effect and clearing his throat noisily, Charlie Roseworthy began to read the article from the paper in a voice which he had borrowed from a visiting actor at the theatre in Chapel Street in Penzance some years earlier.
"Readers will know of that natural curiosity, the Logging Rock at Treen and will share this organ's dismay at the news that the wonder rocks no more. The great stone which was the admiration of every visitor to the Land's End, has been thrown down by the wicked folly of an officer of His Majesty's Revenue Service with the assistance of the crew of his ship, the revenue cutter 'Nimble'. It has been further reported that while this infamy was being perpetrated, a cargo of smuggled goods was being landed in the vicinity, under the very noses of those who's responsibility it was to prevent such vile acts. The name of this officer, commander of the Nimble, has been forwarded to the Admiralty together with a strong letter of complaint and a demand that the stone be set back in its accustomed position with the minimum of delay. The whereabouts of Lt. Hugh Goldsmith are not . . ."

There was uproar at the naming of Hugh Goldsmith. Most of the regular customers had experienced the rough edge of the Lieutenant's tongue while he was staying at the inn. Shortly after the incident of the rock, Hugh Goldsmith had left, rather hurriedly and the Nimble had not been seen at Mousehole since the affair.
"He that was here?" asked old Billy Cocks. "Was it he who scat the rock over?"
"Ess" replied his son, Peter. "Don't it say so in the paper, faither?"
"A viper in our bosoms!" retorted Billy. "What was a snot nosed boy like he doin' disturbin' our ancient monuments what was put there by God Almighty so that

George Harvey and his brothers could make a honest livin'?"
"Ah yes, Billy Cocks" observed Daniel Bone, "but the funny thing is, now the stone is scat down, more visitors than ever have come to see it lying on the ground and to hear the story."
"Matter do uh if they have?" asked Billy. "The fact is, that cocky young booy, who lorded it over all of we in Mousehole, have been and damaged a hainshunt monument and he shouldn't be allowed to get away with it."
"Dosen't ee worry thees self 'bout it, Billy" the landlord told him. "He'll wish his cake dough soon enough. The Penzance magistrates have informed The Admiralty in London and their Lordships are said to be furious about the matter."
"What do ee think will happen to un then Charlie?" asked Peter Cocks.
"I b'lieve they've told Lieutenant Goldsmith that unless he sets matters right, he is going to lose his commission."
"Who's going to lose his commission, Charlie?" asked Nancy Roseworthy, coming up the stairs from the cellar.
"Lt. Goldsmith, Nancy my dear" her husband replied.
"My soul and body!" cried Nancy "what ever for?"
"For scattin' over the Logan Rock and puttin' honest folks up to Treen out of their livelihoods, that's what" cried Billy Cocks.
"I'd never have thought" said Nancy "when he had his supper here the other night that he was planning to do such a wicked thing. He seemed such a fine young gentleman."
"Ess, well" said Peter Cocks "the gentry is always a law unto theirselves, seem to me, and it's we that always has to clear up after their games. How do they think he's going to put that there rock back again? 'Tis easier to scat somethin' over than ee is to heave un back up."
"P'raps ee didn't know the harm ee was doin'. They young fellers from up-long don't seem to knaw much about how the world de turn" said Able Strick.
"I b'lieve he knew well enough Able. He was shamefaced when he came back here that evening." said the landlord and then, mimicking Lt. Goldsmith's way of speaking, added; " 'I think I'd better settle up now, my man. It's been very pleasant here, but one has to move on. The rolling stone gathers no moss, what?' He paid his account and cleared out to Penzance and I had to send his belongings after un to a hotel in Chapel Street."

The conversation continued in this vein for some time. Lt Goldsmith found himself condemned, in his absence, to a damp death in the harbour with a stone around his neck, by the court of the Ship Inn. Nancy, tiring of the conversation, took herself off to bed. The court dealt with several other local difficulties before the members began to drift away to their homes. When Able Strick, always the last to leave, eventually finished his ale and left the bar, Charlie Roseworthy shot the bolts and called out quietly "You there, Dick Richards?"
"Ess I am" came the reply from the shadows. "You took some time getting rid of that Able Strick. I got to get all the way back to Penberth tonight."
"Able?" said Charlie Roseworthy. "Ee de only ever have the one mug of ale and ee de make that last all night but then, he's a lonely old soul and I don't like to

chuck un out."
"You don't do so bad" said Dick. "The rest of the company seems more willing to spend their cash."
"I don't do too bad, Dick" agreed Charlie "but we could do with some more passin' trade, like that Lieutenant Goldsmith, with gold in their pockets instead o' brass."
"Lets hope for some more of they, for both our sakes" said Dick. "Now, I got another cargo in. How much do ee want this time?"
"All that commotion up to Treen is bringing in more visitors these days" mused Charlie. "P'raps I should get a bit of stock in. What you got this time then Dick?"
"Its brandy and rum this time but there's more coming all the time" answered Dick.
"I could do with a few more bottles of that brandy I had last time. The customers did like that. Av ee got any baccy left over Dick?"
"I'll get ee some baccy soon as I can. Now, why don't ee 'av a keg instead of bottles? I could let ee 'av un a bit cheaper."
"Dammee! I don't want no kegs" cried Charlie. "This id'n one of yer spit an' sawdust inns like you got up your way, Dick. My customers are a bit more discerning and like a nice bottle with a proper label on it. I already got the labels printed in Penzance so you keep your kegs and give me bottles or I'll get my brandy from St Just. Now, I'll av a keg or two of rum if you got em. Its only the locals who de drink rum and they don't worry about no bottles."

In a small, rather shabby room on the first floor of a cheap hotel in Chapel Street, Penzance, Hugh Goldsmith was beginning the process of saving his career in His Majesty's navy. There were several pieces of fine writing paper lying, crumpled on the floor. These represented several failed attempts to create the exact tone necessary to extract cash from a small number of individuals. The brevity of the list of possible sources of money was a worry to the young gentleman but, having racked his brains as thoroughly as he could, the list would grow no longer. Now, armed with the best formula he could devise, he resolved to set to work on his correspondence without delay. He sharpened his nib and reached for a fresh piece of letter paper and wrote;

To;
Sir Toby Moss,
White's Club,
London.

My dear Sir Toby,

I write to you in some distress! You may have heard of the trouble associated with the Logan Rock in this district. The press lay the blame for the disaster entirely at my door. In fact the cause of the accident was the overenthusiastic efforts of the brave soldier boys who volunteered to help my scientific investigations. Expert local opinion assured me that no harm could come to the attraction as a result of my proposed investigations

I find myself burdened with the whole of the cost of replacing the rock and have been advised that the alternative would be the loss of my commission. Such an outcome would deal a death blow to my dear mother, the widow of your true friend, my father.

I beg you to come to the aid of your friend's son and relieve my mother's suffering.

I enclose an estimate of the cost of restoring the rock, prepared by local engineers and trust to the Good Lord that you will be able to assist me to discharge this burden.

I remain, Sir, your faithfull servant,
Lt. Hugh Colville Goldsmith RN

The good Lieutenant carefully sanded the paper, read it through and seemed satisfied with this, the first sortie of the campaign. He folded the paper and copied the address from his journal before reaching for a second piece of paper, to be sent to a reverend gentleman of the lieutenant's acquaintance. The basic formula required a little adjustment but soon, a second letter rested upon the first and a third was begun.

By the end of the morning the small heap of letters was ready and Lt. Goldsmith lit the candle and began heating wax. Soon he had sealed each letter with his signet ring and stepped out of the hotel to carry his collection the short distance up the street to the post office. He gave his letters into the hand of the postmaster, paid the necessary postage and, with a heavy heart, returned to his hotel to begin the long wait for his replies.

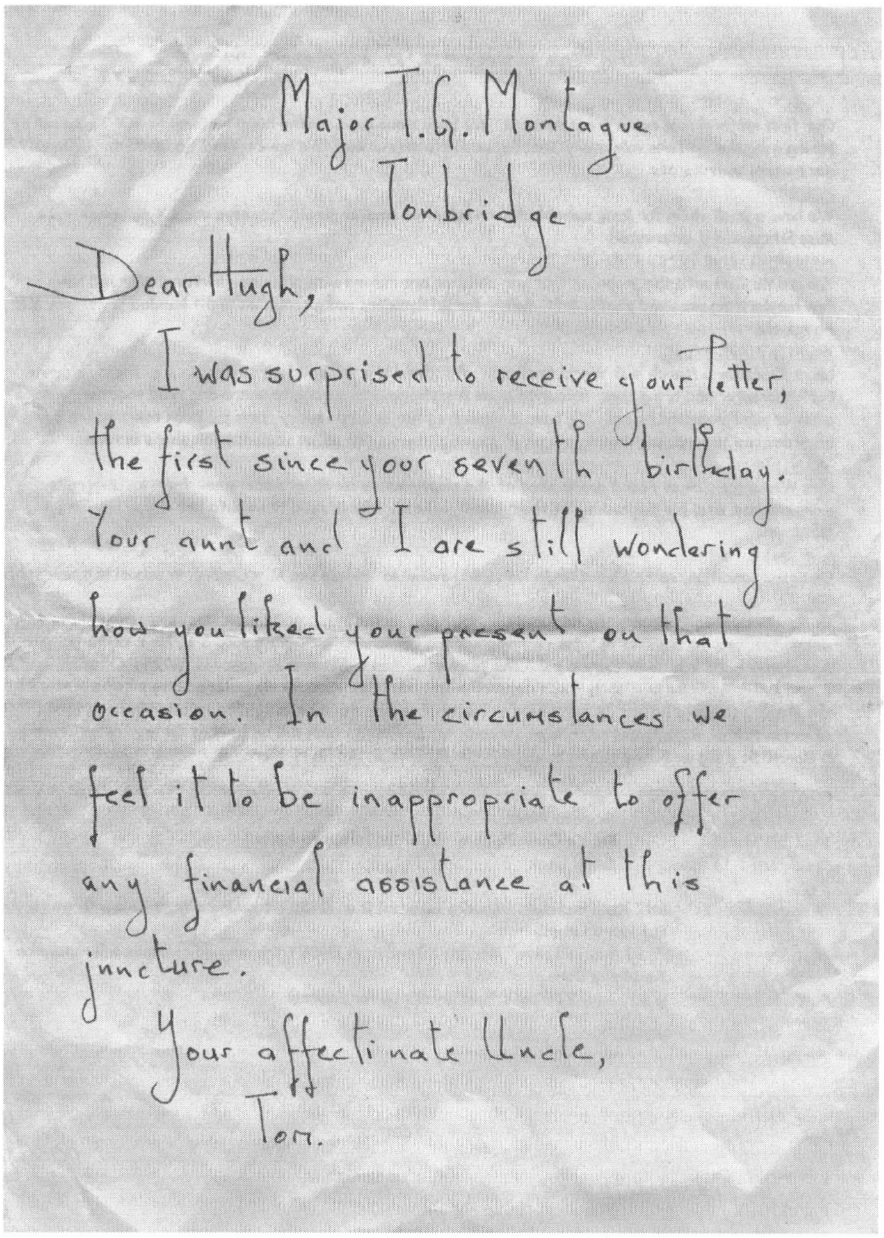

Major T.G. Montague
Tonbridge

Dear Hugh,

I was surprised to receive your letter, the first since your seventh birthday. Your aunt and I are still wondering how you liked your present on that occasion. In the circumstances we feel it to be inappropriate to offer any financial assistance at this juncture.

Your affectionate Uncle,
Tom.

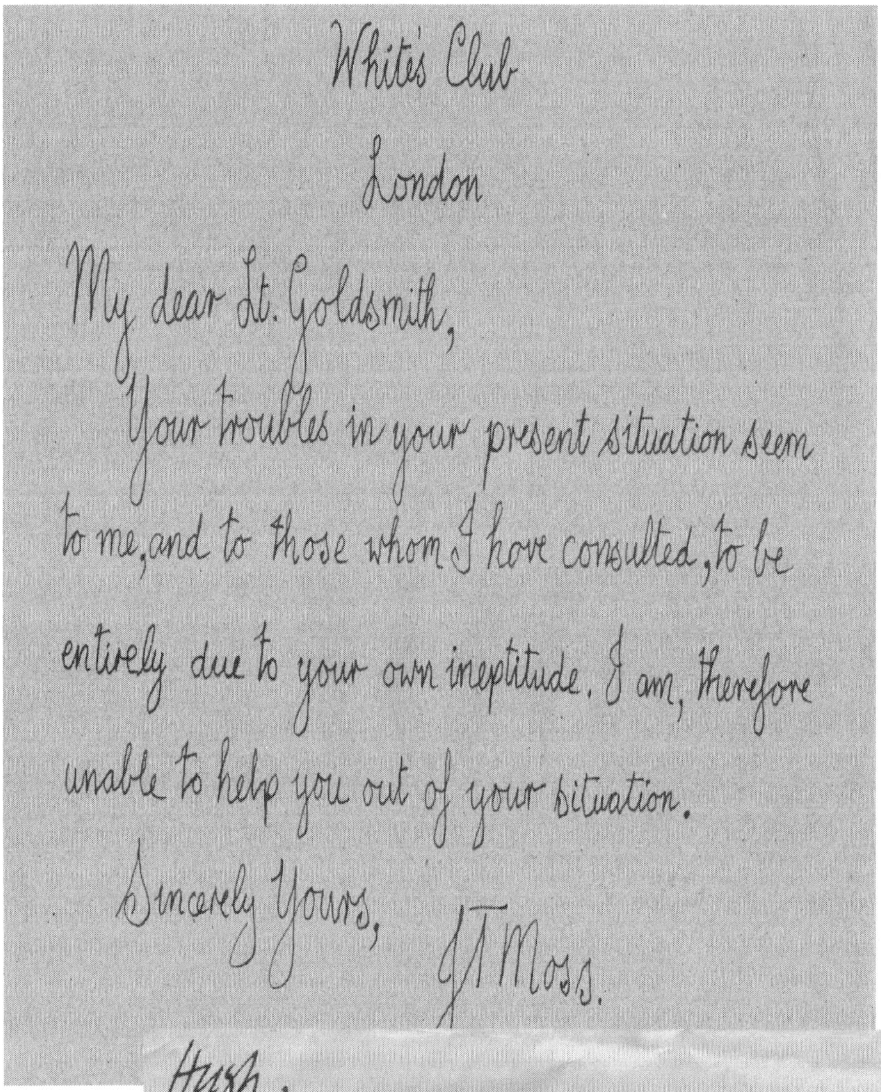

White's Club
London

My dear Lt. Goldsmith,

Your troubles in your present situation seem to me, and to those whom I have consulted, to be entirely due to your own ineptitude. I am, therefore unable to help you out of your situation.

Sincerely Yours,

JT Moss.

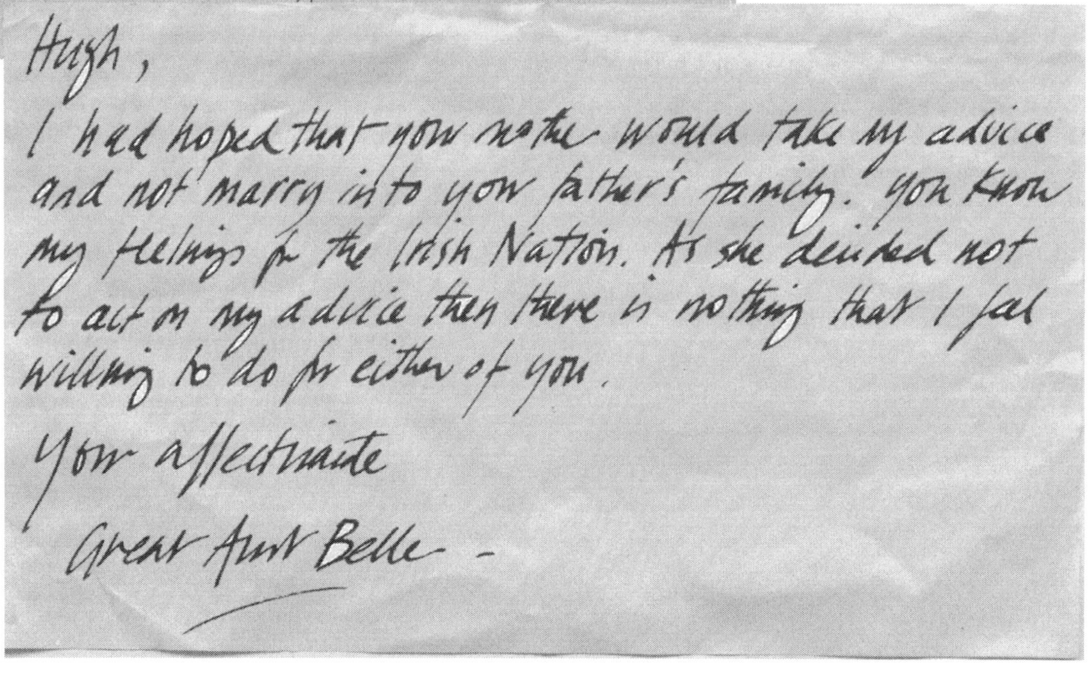

Hugh,

I had hoped that your mother would take my advice and not marry into your father's family. You know my feelings for the Irish Nation. As she decided not to act on my advice then there is nothing that I feel willing to do for either of you.

Your affectionate

Great Aunt Belle -

Jack Tonkin
Greys Inn

Dear Hugh,
Now that school is over, my dear boy, I feel that it would be better if we were to go our separate ways in this world. I hope not to hear from you again

Should you feel the need to write again the I would have no alternative but to persue the matter of

Francis Upton
Cathedral Close

My dear Hugh,
I was so very sorry to hear of your predicament and I only wish that I could help you my dear boy. I am afraid that my living here precludes my being able to assist in a material way but you may be sure that you will feature in my prayers always.
I send my very best regards to your dear mother.
May God bless both of you.
Your Uncle Francis,

And then, when Hugh's optimism had been all but destroyed, came the following letter from Gilbert Davis Esq.

My dear Hugh,

I have read of your troubles in the newspapers and feel heartily sorry for your condition. I feel that you must carry some of the blame for the situation in which you find yourself. However, though your shoulders may be broad enough for physical burdens, they may not carry financial loads so well.

For the sake of your dear mother and for the good name of your father I am willing to underwrite the enterprise but I expect you to repay the loan from your salary. I understand you will have little to spare initially but expect that repayment will accelerate as you advance in the service. Rest assured that I will be watching your progress closely.

Your Friend,

Gilbert Davies

To his credit, on the receipt of this last reply, Hugh Goldsmith fell on his knees and gave sincere thanks to his God and to Mr Gilbert Davies for his deliverance.

Trouble at Treen

It was a fine June morning at Treen and the Harvey brothers were preparing for another busy day, conducting tours around the fallen Logan Rock. Now that work had commenced on restoring the stone to it's former perch, the flow of visitors had increased yet further. It had recently been found necessary to prepare entertainment and refreshment at the inn for those who were waiting for the next tour to begin. George, the inn keeper was down in the cellar and every available member of the Harvey family was busy about the place in stables, kitchens or bed chambers. Only Tom and his brother, Jim Harvey, were in the pot room, waiting for the first visitors to arrive. Jim looked up as the door opened.
"Look, Tom" whispered Jim, "it's that Reuben Richards. What do ee want in 'ere? Ee'd better not be pushin 'is self into our business again."
"We'd best go over and see" said Tom Harvey, rising from his chair. "We don't want Richardses takin what's rightfully ours and what we worked for all this time."
"Well, well!" said Tom, smiling with false bonhomie, "If it isn't the Richardses, comin' over from Penberth to pay us a visit. What ee want in Treen, Reuben?"
"Nothin' more than we de usually want" Reuben answered. "Me and Dick are waiting to see if there be any visitors who want to see the Logan Rock. I hear that there are plenty, now that that Lieutenant Goldsmith and his men have made the place so entertainin'."
"No need to bother, m'son" said Tom. "There wain't be no more than we Harvey brothers can manage, Reuben so you'd better get back to Penberth before you miss the tide 'cos you already missed the boat here my handsome. George is out the back and Arthur is down the cellar so we got enough hands to manage any trade which comes up from Penzance, or from Penberth too, for that matter" he added more menacingly.
"Don't ee get so teasy, Tom" said Reuben trying to calm the situation. "All we want to do is take any you can't manage off yer hands, to ease your burden a bit. Look, here's Dick."

Dick Richards stepped through the doorway, moping his face and panting slightly.
"Sorry to be so long Reuben" he announced, "I had to make a delivery on the way. Good day to you Tom, Jim. Nice lot of visitors today I hope."
"We got 'em all covered Dick" Tom told him. "And George is making sure that any that aren't being shown round by the rest of us are shown proper Treen hospitality here in the Inn. Now, Reuben, your brother 'ere 'ave already said how ee 'ave made a delivery on 'is way ere. That's how you Richards de ply your trade and it's nothing to do with we. Any trouble in that direction is between you and the revenue men. Our trade is peaceful and legal. When we aren't farmin' we're conductin' our visitors round the rock, our rock! Treen, Logan Rock! Nothin' to do with Penberth."

Tom's voice was rising again, together with the colour in his face. Reuben felt the need to reduce the tension in the room.
"Now, now Tom, there's no need get so riled up about it."
"No there isn't" Tom replied "because there's the four of us to the three of you." and then he added, adopting Reuben's approach, "but we aren't really like that, are we Jim?
"No boy, we aren't" said his brother.
"We de like a quiet, peaceful life because that's what the visitors de like too." said Tom.

Reuben forgot his earlier intention to stay calm. "Well we could liven it up a bit if you like Tom 'cos there's plenty of us over to Penberth and us hard from the fishing too, not great soft plough followers and landlords of inns like you Harveys" he taunted.
"No need for you to bluster like that Reuben" said Tom. "None of us wants no trouble. We shall look after all the visitors who de come, just like we de look after the good Lieutenant and his soldiers who de use this place all the time. They're either here or workin' on the rock. The Nimble is the only revenue cutter in these waters and she's anchored here and not likely to move until the rock loggs again. So you two, and Dick there, go back to Penberth, my handsomes, and ply your trade in peace and safety while me and my brothers do the same here. There's no need to be greedy and start fighting for what doesn't concern

you anymore. Anyhow, you know full well that the Nimble could be pointed in your direction by a word from anyone in Treen. Now that would really upset the applecart. I believe even my brother George would be upset if Dick was in Bodmin jail and couldn't deliver his bits and pieces from time to time."
"Cummost on home, boys" said Reuben to his brothers. "It de pain me te say so but there's sense being spoke here and there's a lot of business for us to arrange while the Nimble's tied up.
The Richards clan rose and Reuben held out his hand to Tom who shook it, establishing a wary peace between the Richards and Harvey families, for the time being at least.

Saul had been stationed on the cliff, near the ancient, defensive earthwork known as Treen Castle. His job was to run and tell his family at Penberth if there was any sign of the Nimble moving. The ship had been anchored beneath the cliff for nearly three months now. Three months was a long time for a young lad to lie still and he had found various ways of passing the time more interestingly. He ran errands for the men working on the rock and, in the course of this work, he met the cabin boy of the Nimble who had offered to fight him. The battle had been a close one. Edward Higgins of The Nimble employed the pugilistic skills he had learned aboard ship while Saul Richards of Penberth Cove used the holds and throws of the Cornish style of wrestling. A draw was declared and the two lads became firm friends.

Saul soon realised that he could earn his coppers running errands, enjoy the company of his new friend and still keep an eye on the Nimble. The ship would hardly sail away while part of it's crew remained on shore so, as long as he kept the cabin boy with him, the two could enjoy all those distractions which young lads prefer. It was not long before Saul introduced Edward to the two Nankervis sisters, Sarah and Morwenna, from Porthcurno. Before long Sarah Nankervis and Edward Higgins became a pair and spent many hours wandering the cliff tops alone. This development did not dismay Saul Richards in the least for it left him free to pay court to Morwenna.

The summer passed, love blossomed and the work on the rock progressed. The Nimble remained firmly anchored and the Richards brothers plied their trade and fished between trading trips. The Harveys became expert in the details of the engineering works and passed the information on to countless visitors, some of whom came back two or three times during the season to check progress. Blocks, tackle, ropes and capstans were borrowed from His Majesty's Dockyard. Men were hired. Holes were drilled. Timber was erected. Money was spent and Lieutenant Goldsmith slept very poorly.

"Oh, I'm sure you'll get square one day, Sir" Horace James assured his Lieutenant.
"I'll have to become an admiral first, I should think" Lt. Goldsmith replied ruefully. "And what's that fool doing over there, Mr James? He'll break his neck if he crawls out any further."
"Don't worry sir, he's one of ours, and an expert rigger" The Mate told him. "I'm keeping the men up to the mark, sir. There'll be no larking about I can assure you."
"Glad to hear it" said the Lieutenant.
"Absolutely, sir" said the Mate. "You don't have to worry about the sailors, sir. And I think I've managed to instil some kind of naval discipline into the hired men. The artisans can be relied upon. Each man knows exactly what is required of him."
"And keep those damned visitors back out of the way, man" complained the Lieutenant. "That would really be the finish of me if one of them got themselves crushed."
"Right you are sir" cried the Mate and then, addressing one of the marines, "Jonnah! Get those people back from the rigging and tell Tom Harvey if he can't keep his clients back then I shall close the area to them." The Mate, having dealt with the immediate problems, sought to reassure his Lieutenant further. "Now sir, by the end of today the preparations will be complete. Tomorrow I shall check over every timber, rope, block and capstan myself. If all is well and the weather holds, then we will raise the rock on the following day. It would be as well, however, if we kept the news to ourselves to avoid the whole thing turning into a circus. If we get many more visitors here there won't be room to stand ourselves."
"Very good thinking, Mr James" said the Lieutenant. "Make sure you tell the crew to keep mum."

There was an unusual buzz of excitement in the bar of the Ship Inn on the following Thursday, the day when the paper would be published. Amongst the vast hoards flocking to the rock on the day that the rock was to be lifted, was a reporter from the local paper. A full account of the affair was expected. The process had been long and slow. News began to spread like fire as soon as the fallen stone had begun to stir.

Charlie Roseworthy presided over his bar and was waiting for the moment when his reading of the article would have greatest theatrical effect. Charlie liked to give a good show. The inn door burst open and Able Strick rushed in and pushed his way to the front of the crowd.
"Have it come yet, Charlie?" he asked.
"Have what come, Able?" teased the landlord.
"The newspaper. Have ee got un yet?"
"I got un right here" announced the landlord.

Trouble at Treen

"Is it in"? asked Able.
"Is what in?" the landlord teased again.
"Oh Charlie!" said Nancy his wife, "don't tease poor Able and don't tease the rest of us neither. If you got the paper, read out the news about the rock without delay."
"Very well" said Charlie Roseworthy in his best theatrical voice and a hush fell immediately.
Charlie began to read to an enthralled audience. There was absolute silence during his performance. Every man present relished the firm, oratorical tone of the reader and the flowery style of the account of this momentous happening.

"4:20 pm, Tuesday 2nd November 1824.
The Logan Rock is in it's place and loggs again. By long and arduous perseverance, Lieutenant Hugh Goldsmith and his gallant crew of marines and sailor boys, assisted by many craftsmen and artisans from these environs, has caused to be replaced, that which, by a moment's folly, was cast down in April of this year.

After much careful preparation, a body of sailors manned the capstans and took up the strain. After twenty minutes of Herculean effort there was a cry from the gallant lieutenant "It moves! Thank God!" This was answered with a mighty cheer from the assembled multitude of onlookers."

Charlie enthralled his audience with a stirring account of the worries that the great chains would break and cast the stone down again, wasting many lives as it did so. His description of the slow ascent of the rock until it hung in space a little higher than it's intended perch was thrilling. The moment when the rock was slung sideways before it could be dropped into its final resting place was described so well that most of the jaws in the bar dropped in sympathy.

When George read that "at twenty minutes past four on Tuesday afternoon a signal was given that the rock was in its place, and that it logged again", three cheers were called for by Able Srick and gladly given by the rest of the assembly. As the company at the Ship Inn, Mousehole, rejoiced at the news of his exploits, Lt. Goldsmith was pouring over a very different document in his hotel room in Penzance. It was a detailed account of the costs of the restoration which would have to be repaid to Mr. Davis, his benefactor.

Brought down	£116.5s.8d
Richard Matthews, 1 day's labour	3s.0d
December 31st, Joseph Richards for lodging 5 men for 11 days	19s.4d
The crew of HMS Nimble lodged at Penberth Cove	£1.10s.11d
Mr Paddy, for expense in replacing Mr Batten's timber	15s.3d
January 30th, William Rawlings for drawing crabs and winches from Rock to Penberth	10s.6d
March 3rd Mr Willaim Carnhalls for 20 St Just Men who did nothing but drink beer to the value of	13s.6d
S Boase, blacksmith, repairs to mason's tools	£1.7s.2d
Richard Holmes, shipwright's bill	£7.4s.10d
Paid 2 Penberth men for additional labour	1s.6d
Total	£130 8s 8d

Autumn had faded into winter and the Harvey family was gathered in front of a roaring fire in the Treen Inn.
"Was there many that took rooms at the Inn, George?" asked Tom of his brother, the inn keeper. "Seemed to me there was."
"It picked up a lot when you kept them up to the rock until after the coach to Penzance had left, Tom. We done very well this year and quite a lot of the young ladies said as how they'd like to come back next year. Nothin' to do with you Jim booy I suppose?"
Jim, the youngest Harvey brother and a very handsome lad, coloured a little. "I entertained the visitors in the way that I de knaw best and, if the young ladies liked it, then nobody's complaining."
"Lets hope none of their faithers starts complaining Jim, lad" said George with a grin.
"We didn't see none of they Richards the whole time did us?" observed Tom,

pleased at the outcome of the confrontation earlier in the year.
"Well I did" said George. "Dick Richards was busy as a bee on the road from Penberth and I shouldn' be surprised if that ol' donkey of 'is 'll 'av to go the the knackers after all that struggling up the hill all year, loaded with kegs and bottles. I don't suppose Dick will begrudge the cost of a new one though 'cos he seem to have been busy everywhere for the last few months. Oh ees! An some of they Frenchies come to stay at the Inn as well so, all told, we aven't done too bad boys."

Just around the coast at Penberth Cove a similar meeting of the Richards clan was discussing the year's activities. Dick Richards was worried about the future.
"Reuben, booy, I de knaw trade been good this year but how we goin' to manage, now that the rock is loggin' again and the Nimble is back on the prowl? We got te eat this winter and the fishing idn't goin' te keep us."
Reuben smiled and winked at Saul. The two had been out in the boat that afternoon and Saul had given his uncle some interesting news.
"You tell un Saul, boy" said Reuben to his nephew.
"Well, Uncle Dick" said the boy "you mind I was up near the rock keeping an eye out while the Nimble crew was workin?"
"Ess lad, I do" answered his uncle. "What do that 'ave to do with the price of fish?"
"I got friendly with the cabin boy off the boat."
"Well, what about un?" said Dick roughly.
"Leave the lad tell 'is tale, Dick" said Reuben. "go on, booy."
"Well," said Saul. "Edward was too small for the work on the rock and the soldiers told un he was in the way and not doin' no good. They said he should fetch croust and carry messages for them all instead. Well they soon forgot all about un and we went off together to 'av a bit of fun."
Dick became impatient with the lad's story again. "I don't see as how all this ..."
Reuben winked at Saul again. "You just hear the lad out, Dick. Its some 'ansome!" he said with a laugh.
"You knaw they two Nankervis maids at Porthcurno, Uncle Dick? Well, Sarah took a real fancy to young Edward, and ee to 'er as well."
"Well, what of ..."
"Tell im, Saul, lad" said Reuben, eager to see his brother's face when he heard Saul's news.
"Edward has te let me know whenever the Nimble is in these parts so that I can tell Sarah and she can go up the cliffs and wave to un. We de get te knaw 'zackly where the cutter is when she's likely te interfere with trade."
There was a short pause and then a broad grin spread over Dick's face and all the Richards brothers burst out in a roar of laughter.
"Well, dang me, my bucca" cried Dick Richards as soon as he caught his breath again, "that's neat as a robin that is. Us shain't starve after all. Well done Saul, lad."

There was yet another business meeting that week, a small one between the landlord and landlady of the Ship Inn, Mousehole.
"Our drapes are some shabby, Charlie. This Inn is getting to be a shabby as me. Everythin' seem to be wearing out" Nancy Roseworthy complained.
"All right Nancy, my bird" said her husband, "you shall have your new drapes and while you're about it, why not pay that Miss Penhale a visit too."
A puzzled look came over Nancy's face. "The dressmaker?" she said, "why should I want to visit she?"
"So you can take her down a peg, the snotty nosed baggage" said her husband with a grin.
"How am I going to do that, Charlie?" asked his wife. "Every time I have to see she, she de make me feel some small. She de always think that I'm going to have a gown made in the fancy stuff she do use for the gentry and she de know very well we can only afford one made from..."
"Silk" announced Charlie softly.
"Silk!" cried his wife. "Now don't you go making me feel as small as she do Charlie. We cain't afford no silk as well you know."
"You shall have silk this time, my handsome" said Charlie, proudly. "And you shall go to Paul Church at Christmas and shame all they other hoity-toity baggages into the bargain. We done very well this year. Lots of they visitors to the Logan Rock who couldn't get places in Penzance come here. And very free spenders some of them were too. Some said that the wines here were the best in the district."

"That's because you didn't deal with they Richards, Charlie. Their wines and spirits are tainted by smuggling and you only gets quality if you buys legal like I always told you."
"Ees, well uh!..." stuttered Charlie, somewhat shamefacedly. "I spose you're right there Nancy."
"A silk gown!" cried the ecstatic Nancy. "Oh! I never dreamed that I would ever have one of they. Oh Charlie, my handsome, silk! And silk drapes too!"
"Well, Nancy! I aren't so sure about silk drapes as well my dear." said the landlord.

Lt. Hugh Colville Goldsmith R.N. received no further advancement in the service and died at sea off St Thomas in the West Indies, in October 1841.

The Magic Potion

"I b'lieve you're a witch, Granny" said Tom.
"Dosen't ee be so plum, boy" the old lady replied.
"Ess you are" the lad insisted. "Mrs. Harris next door said as how you addled all her chickens' eggs because you and she had words."
"Mrs Harris have got a voice on her that would addle adder's eggs" his granny announced. "She don't need no witch. If her eggs was harmed then it was her own fault, the spiteful old soul."
"But they de all bullyrag me up to school about it Granny" wailed the boy. "They de all say as how you're a witch and if I aren't careful then you shall turn me into somethin' slimy like a quilken. What is a quilken anyway?"
"Its what we used to call a frog years ago" answered the old lady. "Now, Tom boy, they de only say things like that to ee because you're simple enough to leave 'em do it. You got to stand up for yerself, my handsome."
"Couldn't you put a spell on 'em for me gran?"
"How's that standin' up fer yerself?" his granny asked him. "And anyhow, I told ee, I aren't no witch. Mind you," mused the old lady, the germ of an idea swelling in her mind, "it de all depend on what you de mean by 'a witch' I s'pose." The old woman gazed out of the tiny cottage window and into the bright sunlight flooding her little garden with spring freshness.
"I knew it! I knew you was" cried the boy, triumphantly. "Do some magic for me Gran, somethin' te frighten they big boys up school and make they leave me alone."

His grandmother regarded the boy, her daughter's only child, and felt a surge of love and pity for him. He was the image of his father and he seemed to have inherited many of Tom's other characteristics as well. Tom Hocking had been almost too timid to woo Penny Tregurtha. Penny had needed to work very hard to give him the opportunities and the encouragement necessary to approach the idea of marrying her. The whole village was amazed to learn that such a shy young man had courted and won one of the prettiest girls in the district. Marriage, a son and all the associated responsibilities had hardened Tom a little. He surprised the whole village by declaring that he would join the Merchant Navy to provide more of a life for his family than his job in the book shop could ever be expected to. Penny and Tom were considerably better off financially but they both missed the man in their lives more than he could have expected. Granny Tregurtha

found herself taking on part of the role of husband and father to the pair.
'I ought to do something to help the lad' thought Tom's Granny and then she told him "Now, me son, you tell me what magic is and I shall tell ee if I'm a witch or no or if I can do magic or no."
"Magic, Gran? Well that's easy enough."
"Go on then" said his granny, "tell me what ee is then."
A puzzled look spread over Tom's face as he pondered the question. "I s'pose ee's doin' something nobody else can do."
"Like jumpin' six foot in the air I s'pose?" asked Granny.
"No, that's not what I meant at all, Gran. More like doing the impossible, making things disappear"
"Like on the stage down the Pavilion Theatre, in Penzance last Christmas you mean?" asked the old lady.
"Not really, everybody de knaw that that's only tricks" said young Tom.
"P'raps that's what magic is, just tricks" said his granny. "If that's all ee is, then I am a witch! I got lots of tricks up my sleeve."
"Have you Gran, really?" said the lad enthusiastically. "Go on then."
"Go on what?"
"Do one of the tricks, the ones you got up your sleeves" begged the boy.
"You cain't just do 'em" said Granny, beginning to enjoy the situation and eager to please the boy with an idea which had occurred to her. "The time got to be right for one thing and you got to have the right magical things to do the tricks with."
"What you got to have, Granny? Cain't we go an' get 'em?" begged Tom, enthusiasm bringing a flush to his pale complexion. "What de ee need? I shall go out an' fetch 'em for ee."
"You're altogether too hasty, young Tom. The potion I got in mind has to be made between May Day and Midsummer. Cain't be made no other time.
"Why not Gran?"
"You got to pick the flowers between those days or the magic won't work."
"What sort of flowers?"
"Wiffy bush flowers"
"Do they smell nice?"
"I wouldn't say nice exactly" said Tom's granny.
"Can we get them today?"
"Not today, me son, they got to be wide open with the sun on em and wiffy bush flowers are only in bud at the moment"
"But will they be out in time? Midsummer must be soon."
"If we're intended to succeed with our potion then they'll be out in time. If we aren't then they shain't."
"But that de mean that I shain't be able to tell nobody up school what I'm goin' to do and they shain't be scared of me 'cos I'm a witch, Gran."
"You aren't no witch, Tom boy. You cain't be cos you haven't done no magic yet, have ee?"
"No Gran."
"And if you was a witch, (or a pellor, which is the right name for a 'wise man' round here, even if some some *do* call 'em wizards), If you was a pellor then best not to let nobody know 'til you're a real good one. If you was to let on before that then the bullyraggin' would get worse and worse and the potion wouldn't

do ee no good at all."
"I got to keep it secret, Gran?"
"Ess you have my son. You don't hear me shoutin' about me bein' a witch, do ee?"
"No, s'pose" was Tom's sulky reply.

"First off" said the old lady "best thing would be to cultivate 'the look'."
"The look, Gran? What's the look?"
"You got to practice that young Tom. That look is one of the most important thing for a young pellor to get right, if he don't want no more bullyraggin' up school that is. Here's yer first lesson, young Tommy booy. You de need just the littlest hint of a smile. No, my handsome! That's a git grin that is. Hardly no smile at all is best, and then look off a bit in the distance and maybe a bit of a 'hmmm' to yerself as you de walk away from the bullyraggin. Most important of all is not to take no notice of what they're sayin' to ee at all. Right, my handsome?" And then the old lady surprised the boy by shouting at the top of her voice, imitating the lads tormentors. "Your granny's a witch, Tom. Your granny's a witch!"
Tom looked at his granny in amazement.
"Come on, my son, what have ee got to do?"
Tom slowly realised what was expected of him. He made his first attempt at 'the look'.
"Too much smile" was granny's response. He tried again.
"That's better, now, look off into the distance. Your granny's a witch! What have ee got to say about that then?"
"No she idn't?" asked the boy.
"You aren't thinking boy! Come on, what did I just tell ee?"
"Oh ess! I remember now. Hmmm."
"That's right and then just turn and stroll away."
"Do ee think it'll work, Granny?" asked the worried boy, thinking of the ordeals he had endured the previous week at school.
"Maybe not right away, Tom, my golden, but magic id'n like that, ee de take time to work, 'specially when you're just startin' out and haven't got hardly no skills yet. Now, leave us try again."

Monday evening came and the old lady was sipping her tea when the door burst open and banged against the wall as Tom flew into the cottage.
"Ee worked, Gran! Ee worked. The magic worked."
"Told ee it would, didn' I? Now, shut the door home and come and tell me all about un, my bird."
"I done what you said" cried Tom. "I just did the look and then wandered away. I thought ee wouldn' work at all at first cos they just kept on shoutin 'Tom's

granny's a witch, Tom's granny's a witch' but I did what you said again a couple of more times and they stopped. Ee was magic, Gran, magic. They just stopped.
"What did I tell ee my golden? That's the power of the old look I told ee about. That old look just told 'em they wasn't goin' to get no fun out of Tom Hocking no more. That old look said 'leave us go off and bullyrag somebody else a bit more interesting instead'. Might not work every time but ee's easy to do, once you had a bit of practice and ee don't do no harm do uh?"
"Can we make the potion now, Gran? Can we do it today? Anyhow, what does it do, this potion we're goin to make?"
"Come back Saturday afternoon and we shall have a go, booy Tom" said his granny. If the sun is out and I got the other magic ingredients, then we shall have a go at makin' un then."
"But what does it do, Granny? Does it make things disappear?"
Granny laughed and shook her head. "No, it doesn't 'zactly do that Tom but it can make you happy and it can make you sad and it might even make you ill if you were very foolish. It all depends on how you use it. And don't ee go getting too excited, my bird, cos Rome wasn't built in a day and this potion isn't neither. You got to prepare things in advance in the magic trade, my handsome, and this potion wain't be ready for six months or more. You got to gather the flowers before the longest day and not use the potion until after the shortest day and that's just before Christmas."
"My gar, Granny. I got job enough to not get too excited about Christmas already and now I got my first potion to look forward to as well."
"Now you done very well, learning the look, and that seem to have worked. The next lesson you got to learn is much harder than that Tom boy."
"Dosen't ee worry, Granny, I shall learn un proper job" said the boy.
"Well, here's the next lesson. You don't tell nobody about what you've learned and you keep yer excitement to yerself so that nobody de guess that somethin's up and start bullyraggin of ee again to find out what ee is."
"Alright Gran. I shain't tell nobody, nobody at all. Now, what's the next lesson?"
"That was it my handsome" said his granny. "You just had un."

Tom managed somehow to get through the rest of the week without blurting out that he was being trained as a pellor by his granny, who was a witch, and they were going to make his first potion at the weekend. Whenever the bullies targeted him, he remembered 'the look' and they soon became bored with the unresponsive boy and moved onto more entertaining targets. Eventually, Saturday came. Tom did his weekend chores as fast as he was able, rushed his lunch and ran out of the house, shouting to his mother that he was 'just up Gran's' and would be 'back in time for tea'.

"Is it sunny enough, Gran?" cried the boy as he burst into his grandmother's cottage. "Have ee got all the other things you de need?"

The Magic Potion

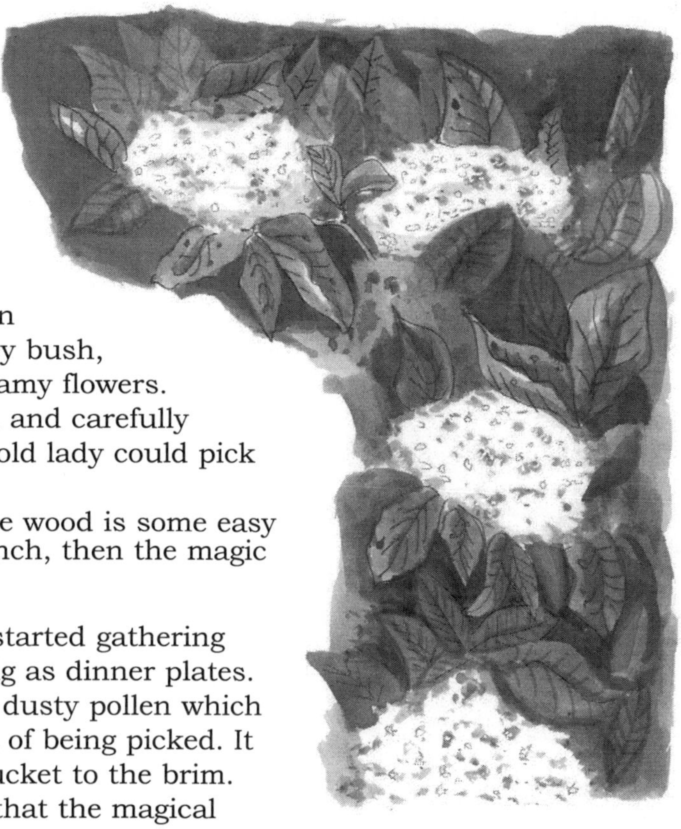

"I b'lieve ee's just about sunny enough and the flowers is wide open, I checked in the week and they should be just right this afternoon. Now, boy Tom, you grab that there bucket and off we go."

The two walked a short distance down the lane until they came upon a wiffey bush, its branches laden with sprays of creamy flowers. Tom was told to put his bucket down and carefully bend the branches down so that the old lady could pick the sprays.
"Now you be careful, Tom boy, cos the wood is some easy to break and if you de snap off a branch, then the magic wain't work."

Tom did as he was told and Granny started gathering flower heads which were almost as big as dinner plates. Her hands were soon yellow with the dusty pollen which burst from the sprays with the shock of being picked. It took a mere five minutes to fill the bucket to the brim. Tom experienced a mixture of regret that the magical experience was over so soon and an eagerness to get back to the cottage to start work on the potion.
"Fill the big kettle from the bussa, Tom, and put un on the slab to boil. We're goin to make a pot of tea."
"Cain't we do the potion first Granny? I only just had my dinner and I don't want no tea yet."
"Dosen't ee be so plum, boy" said his granny, "the tea is goin' in the potion and lots of other ordinary things too. But I got one real magic ingredient in the spence. You shall have the honour of puttin' that in when the time de come."

A huge pot of very strong tea was prepared and then more water was put on the slab to boil. Lemons were squeezed and, to Tom's surprise, the juice was added to the tea pot. As soon as the water had boiled it was poured over the flowers in the bucket and then the lemony tea was added to the brew.
"This is some queer" said Tom, "we de generally have our tea with milk and sugar up home."
"Lots of people de have their tea with lemon" said Tom's granny "and I shall be addin' sugar in a minute but I aren't goin' to use no milk. You go out to the scullery boy and bring in the big glass jars out there. They're all clean as clean and I don't want you making them dirty again so you give your hands a good wash before you go."

The boy did as he was told and brought the four huge jars from the larder and placed them on the well scrubbed kitchen table. Granny produced a large glass funnel and placed it into the first jar. A muslin cloth was placed in the funnel and the infusion of flowers with its strong tea and lemon juice was strained into the container. There was some liquid remaining and this was strained into a second container. The kettle was refilled and put to boil once more on the slab. Granny then set to work, distributing the murky looking mixture amongst the jars until the height of liquid in each was identical.

"Don't we need no magic words Gran?" asked Tom.
"No need, boy" she replied "We picked the flowers on the right day and we used all the right things for the potion. That'll be fitty enough."
"What else we got to put in Gran?"
"I told ee, young Tommy, sugar's next."
"Sugar don't sound very magic, Gran" said the boy. "We got tea and lemon and a few flowers which smell a bit stinky to me. And you haven't said no special words. Where's the magic in that lot?"
"That's right Tommy" his granny replied "all the ingredients in magic spells, they're very ordinary but the magic is coming lad. You just wait. But first we need the very last thing on the list in the grimoir. There now, that's a word idn' uh? Grimoir, is that magic enough for ee?"
"Oh ess, Gran. That's a real magic word. Almost as magic as abracadabra that is. What do it mean?"
"Book of spells" said Granny, laughing.

The old lady had been enjoying teasing the boy about his enthusiastic acceptance of everything she had told him about the magical recipe. The look of disappointment on the lad's face caused the old lady to take the whole thing more seriously.
"That last ingredient is the most magical of all, Tom booy. And like many a magical item ee don't look nothin' out of the ordinary. Ee's the sort of thing most folks would throw away and never give a minute's thought to."
"What is uh, Granny?" Tom asked, his enthusiasm for the spell rekindled.
"Ee's out the Spence in the old wine

bottle. Fetch un for me now booy. The time'll soon be right."
"This bottle here?" called the lad from the larder. "There idn' nothing but a drop in the bottom, Gran."
"Ee'll be enough for what we de want, Tom. That drop is the spirit of the wine, the essence you might say. That's the magical ingredient all right so footch un out here."

The bottle was brought and placed carefully on the dresser. Granny brought out the scales and weights and then started to weigh a surprising quantity of sugar into the first of two large bowls, one of which was placed in front of Tom. Hot water from the kettle was poured onto the sugar and then cold water from the bussa was added until the bowls were almost full. Granny produced two large spoons and gave one to the boy.

"Stir" said the old lady.
"How long for?" asked Tom.
"'Til all the sugar's gone" his granny replied. "I s'pose ee wain't hurt if you de want to say a few magic words but I don't s'pose they'll do no good neither. Knaw any magic words do ee?"
"No" said Tom.
"Don't ee bother then but keep on stirrin' and dosen't ee go splashin' of un all over the table. That sugar been very carefully measured, that have, and we don't want to spoil the spell do us?"

It took a great deal of stirring before Granny was satisfied that all the sugar had been dissolved. The funnel was placed in the first of the four glass jars. When all the sugar water had been added, cold water was added until the jar was nine tenths full. The second glass jar was treated similarly and then the whole dissolving process was repeated for the remaining jars.

"Time for you to go home to yer mother now, Tom" his granny told him.
"Oh Gran!" cried the boy. "You said I could put the magic stuff in."

"Oh ess, so I did, lad" said Granny kindly. "Here, pass be the bottle from the dresser and that little jug there."

Granny filled the jug with cold water from the big earthenware bussa and added it to the wine bottle before giving it a good shake.

"Here you are Tom" she said, passing him the bottle. "Pour a quarter of that into each jar. That's the last of the spell and we shall have to sit back and wait until Christmas to see how well the magic works."
"Christmas, Gran! I cain't wait til Christmas" wailed the lad.
"Then thees'll just have to, my handsome! I told ee it would be a long old haul, this magic potion. Never mind my robin, Come and see yer old granny next Saturday and you shall have a bit of a surprise and I shall give ee yer next bit of training to be a pellor.

Tom did as he was asked and walked off home with the stern reminder from his granny ringing in his ears. "Now, Tom, like all magic and wishes and such, these things de only work if you de keep 'em to yerself. So don't ee go shoutin' yer mouth off to nobody about yer lessons up here with yer Granny, not even yer mother and certainly not they bullyboys up to school. Just remember 'the look' and don't give 'em nothing to make it worthwhile bullyraggin of ee."

Tom did as he was told and the advice certainly seemed to work. At least once a week he visited his granny and each time he wanted to check how the potion was developing. At first he was impressed to see it become a seething, murky mess which fizzed and popped. Later, the bubbling gradually slowed and the liquid began to clear. One week, when the bubbling seemed to have stopped completely and Tom believed the magic to have gone out of the mixture altogether, everything changed. The pale gold liquid was sitting in fresh, clean jars. All the sludge at the bottom had gone and the potion was crystal clear.
"She's almost ready now, booy Tom" his granny said to him as he admired the row of sparkling vessels. "Come Christmas she'll be out of they jars and into nice clean bottles, all corked up ready for the season."
"How long is it to Christmas now, Granny?" asked Tom.
"You de knaw so well as I do, Tom. Four weeks next Wednesday. I shall come to yours for Christmas day and you shall come up here, Boxing day for your tea with the rest of the crew."
"And when shall we use the potion, Granny?" asked Tom.
"Boxing Day, like I said" she told him.
"I still don't know what its going to do" said Tom. "What's going to happen, Gran? Is it going to be magic?"
"You just wait and see, my handsome" said his granny.
"I got a hard job, waitin' for Christmas this year, Gran" said Tom.
"Why this year in particular, Tom boy?" asked his Granny.
"Mum told me, this morning Gran. My daddy's comin' home for Christmas."
"Oh my dear lamb!" cried Tom's granny as she grabbed the lad and hugged him tight. "That's the best bit of news I've had for I don't know how long."

There were three things for Tom to look forward to, Christmas, his magic brew and his daddy's home coming. He simply had to be patient. It is difficult to remember just how hard it is for a young boy of eight or nine to to be patient. All of us have experienced the agony but few can remember its intensity. Somehow, Tom managed to continue existing until Christmas morning when he received his presents. Some were disappointingly practical but in the main he was very pleased with the contents of the pillowslip which he found on his bed post that morning. When he went downstairs for his breakfast, there was his father, sitting at the head of the table, in his old place, looking tanned and smiling broadly.
"Daddy!" cried the boy, running across the kitchen to throw himself into his father's arms. Unable to help himself, he burst into tears. Soon all three, father, mother and son were standing in the kitchen, hugging, laughing and crying together. It was some time before Tom's mum remembered the breakfast on the stove and ran off to save it from disaster. Christmas day passed in a haze of

love, excitement, feasting and merriment. Tom forgot his potion and his magical training, even when Granny turned up just before the Christmas dinner was served.

Boxing Day morning meant visits to cousins and sharing their toys and playing games with uncles. Eventually, the whole family decamped and set off to visit Tom's granny who had another vast spread ready for them to enjoy. It was only when he entered Granny's cottage that the old preoccupation with the effects of his potion returned. Tom cornered the old lady to ask the inevitable question.
"When are we going to ...?" he began.
"Right away, Tom boy" she interrupted him. You go and get one of the bottles out to the spence and I shall bring a tray full of glasses into the parlour. And I mustn't forget the corkscrew."

Everyone had settled into the tiny parlour when Tom arrived holding one of the bottles of the golden potion. The whole family had managed to find seats somewhere in the little room and each had been supplied with a glass by Tom's granny.
"Ah!" cried Tom's dad. Here's the boy with the bottle. Give un to yer granny Tom. We're all sitting here with our tongues hanging out."
Tom handed the bottle to his granny to open and the lad wondered why the whole family, especially his dad, whom he had believed to be a very sensible individual, were so keen on drinking the magic potion. Granny pulled the cork out with a satisfying 'pop' and the liquid glug-glugged into the glasses. Everyone took a sip.

"Better every year, Gran" cried Tom's dad. "My gar! I been lookin' forward to this all the time I been away."
"Not been lookin' forward to seein' me then?" teased Tom's Mum.
"Almost as much" laughed Tom's dad. "Your gran, Tom," he continued "she makes the best wine in the whole of Cornwall."
"Wine!" cried Tom, "but I thought it was a mag ..."
"My best elderflower wine, Tom" interrupted his granny.
"But where's the magic in that?" asked Tom, clearly disappointed after his six month long wait for something spectacular.
"Your old Gran? She's magic sure enough Tommy" said his dad with a grin. "Her wine de knock spots off any boughten wine you can get down to Harveys, the wine merchants, don't uh, Mother?"
"Ess, I b'lieve you're right" answered his mother in law. "Mind you I had some years of practice now and you'll be pleased to know that when I'm dead and gone, you shall still have a decent drop of stuff at Christmas and into the New Year too."
"How's that Mother?" asked Tom's dad. "I hope you aren't thinking of goin' up the church yard in the near future" he added.
"I aren't in no violence to get up there my son" said the old lady "but even so, I s'pect I shall be there a good while before you are. No, what I de mean is that I've taken on an apprentice. Young Tom there, he helped me to make the wine this year and I shall teach un a bit more about it next year. You wait! Soon enough he shall be makin' wine so good as mine and different sorts too. With any luck, when he's old enough to drink more than a thimbleful himself, he'll be the family brewer sure enough."
"Well now, who would have thought? You're a dark horse sure enough, Tom" said his mother, looking proudly at the boy.

The party settled down and a second and a third bottle of magic potion was broached and enjoyed. Tom remained quiet for half an hour, an unusual condition for the young lad. His granny, noticing that the boy didn't seem to be taking his usual enthusiastic part in the occasion, asked Tom to 'give her a hand in the kitchen'.

"Now then, whassamatter with ee, boy?" she enquired.
"Nothing."
"Ess there is" the old lady insisted. "You seem a bit teasy to me, my handsome. Tell me what's bothering ee."
"I thought it was going to be real magic, Gran. But ee waddn' nothing but wine after all. I been waitin' for months and now ee don't seem to be worth it at all."

The Magic Potion

"Now then, me son" said his granny, "it all depends on what you think magic is. My wine is magic enough if you think what ee can do. A little drop like you had is nice and warming and makes ee feel nice and relaxed. A drop more and you start kiheakin' about the place, makin' a fool of yourself. A drop more than that and it de make ee feel very bad. There now, what else de have such effects in a little glass? The party's goin' with a swing like they de say and I shain't leave nobody drink too much, 'specially yer uncle Arthur who seem to have a great susceptibility to the old potion. He de get a bit leary and starts botherin' the ladies if you de let un. And now, booy, you are in training to take over as family brewer and you can soon do all the magic yourself. And don't ee think that's all the magic I'm goin' to teach ee my son. There tons more and I shall tell ee all I de knaw."
"But are they real magic, Granny or just the same as the old wine?"
"You aren't listenin' to me booy, you can do somethin' now that nobody else in the family de knaw how to do and soon enough, you shall learn how to do lots of other things in the same way. Now, Id'n that magic? Bein' able to do what other folks can't do and wishes they could?"
"Ess, I s'pose" said Tom unconvinced.
"And didn't I do the magic to get rid of they bullyboys up school?"
"Ess, I s'pose" was the surly reply.
"No 'I s'poses' about it at all" said the old lady. "Now, cheer up and I'll leave ee have a drop more of the potion, if they've left any that is. Only a drop mind cos ee's strong old stuff that elderflower wine and I don't want you makin' a hexhibition of yerself like poor old Arthur."

Tom took his second, small glass of wine and, this time he sipped it slowly and soon he found that the old lady was right. He really did feel more relaxed and less 'teasy'. The taste was unusual, like nothing he had ever tasted before. It wasn't sweet as he had always assumed wine would be and what exactly *was* the taste of it? It was certainly nothing like the slightly unpleasant smell of the flowers in the bucket, that June afternoon, so long ago now. The best Tom could do was describe the taste to himself as the taste of the sunny afternoon, the freshness of the early summer and the smell of a Cornish hedgerow, bursting with wild flowers with a promise of blackberries to come.

He looked across at his uncle Arthur and realised that Granny was right again. Arthur had commandeered a bottle of 'potion' all to himself and was behaving very oddly. Perhaps magic was simply doing ordinary things that ordinary people thought they couldn't do. Granny's solutions to problems were very sensible and they worked very well. Perhaps she was right and, if he stuck to his apprenticeship lessons, maybe he could become the family pellor after all.

Saints

Some time after the creation and the fall, humanity had followed the instruction to 'go forth and multiply' with enthusiasm. The result was, lots of people but nobody quite sure who belonged where. It fell to God to sort it all out and so He called all the people on earth together for a meeting.

The BIG SHARE-OUT was to take place outside the old Garden of Eden which had been closed down ages ago. Those who come early ended up near the front of the queue. Those who had other things to worry about, like Ives did and Dennis did and Hayle and Penzance, they couldn't just go off to some land share-out at the drop of a hat. They had broccoli to cut and taties to teal. So when they eventually arrived, the end of the queue was miles away from the garden and they were last!

Dennis and Erth got 'bream teasy', thinking about all the jobs at home that weren't getting done. But then Agnes joined the boys and soon settled them down. Always a calming influence was Agnes. Soon they decided on *inventing* as a means of passing the time. Inventing was a very popular pastime in those days because nothing much had been invented yet!

Dennis said it was his idea, but Austell disagreed. Whoever it was, one of them had the idea of a PUB. It was such a good idea that the boys started work, building one straight away. Agnes wasn't much of a one for the building so she invented beer instead. She put on a brew so that it would be ready by 'croust'. It was handsome, they all agreed that. Agnes said it wouldn't take her long to make a few more gallons for the evening and so the others got back to work.

Our boys soon forgot all about the big share-out. There was God, doling out the lands and Agnes and the boys were talking no notice at all. They were all inside the pub, as soon as it had its roof on, enjoying the delights.

Gradually, each tribe got its own part of the world and was content, more or less, for the time being, anyway. And God saw what He had done and saw that it was good. He was quite pleased with Himself. Somehow though, it didn't feel quite finished. God had a mental check through the day and... He was right! He couldn't remember seeing Ives, or Dennis or Hayle or their mates. He wondered what had happened and decided to seek them out. And then there was Agnes! He hadn't seen Agnes all day either and he was worried about her too.

He looked and looked - and then he saw it - He hadn't made *that.* It was *much* too regular, and too pointy, with smoke coming out of it. Not His style at all. God would have made a much better job of a volcano than that. It should be much bigger for a start. And then he saw the door and, being God, He knew the right thing to do, straight off. He knocked.

God hammered on the door a bit harder than He intended because He hadn't had much practice at door knocking. It certainly frightened the pub customers to death, great booming knocks like that, in the middle of the night. Agnes said that, as Ives was the biggest, he ought to go. Cautiously, slowly, Ives cracked open the door and there, silhouetted against the full moon was the biggest pair of hippy sandals containing the biggest pair of feet in creation.

"Well, well" said God. "What ee all doin in 'ere?"

"Its our pub" said Erth.

"We invented it" said Dennis.

"Come in and sit down" said Ives.

"Penzance will get ee a chair" said Agnes.

"No ee wain't," said Erth, "Ee an Hayle said they wadn't feelin well and went 'ome."

How He did it, nobody ever knew but God, who was much bigger than the pub while He was outside, just walked in and made Himself at home.

"This is some nice" He said "but what do ee do in here?"

"We de drink this" said Agnes. "Try some, its handsome."

God tried the beer and He was very impressed. "It's a lot different from the water I created" He said, "got more body to it."

"That was Agnes" said Dennis. "She created beer."

"She *invented* it" said God, "lets maintain some demarcation here. Now, this pub, or what you de call it, whose idea was that?"

Ives said that they had all "crea.... invented it."

"This is splendid", said God. "This is making more of creation than was given to ee. I would never have made such a regular construction with its straight walls and its pointy roof."

"And the chimney" said Erth, "that was my bit."

"And the chimney" said God. "Well done my ansomes! And this beer, cheers ee up rich after a hard day's work and I bet it de give ee a good night sleep too."

"Ess" said Agnes, a bit concerned. "But you might have to get up once or twice before morning!"

"A minor problem, nothing is perfect. Tell ee what", said God, mellow now and feeling more benevolent than usual, which was extremely benevolent! "You lads, and you too Agnes, you need some sort of reward for this work you done, developing creation and making something special. Now, I shall have to invent something."

"Don't you mean create something" said Erth.

"Don't you be cheeky", said God "or I shall think again about ... making you all saints."

Saints

"Saints!" said Agnes. "You hear that Ives. You're a saint."

"Saint Ives!" he replied.

"And I'm Saint Agnes" she said. "I de like the sound of that. But what about old Penzance an' Hayle?"

"What about em?" asked God.

"They goin to be saints?" asked Saint Agnes.

"Did they 'ave anything to do with inventing the pub?" asked God.

"No, they left early" she replied.

"Best not then," said God, "Well now! I'd better be off home to 'eaven. I'm feelin' a bit 'eadlight after that beer of yours, Saint Agnes."

"Good night's sleep will sort ee out fitty, you'll see" said Saint Agnes.

"Hang about a minute," said Saint Erth. "Dosn't ee rush off. Where we goin to live? We never got nowhere in the share-out."

"I don't know if there's anywhere left" said God, sounding a bit worried. "Leave me av a geek in the ol' golden horn and see." He looked and then he turned it upside down and gave it a shake. Out tumbled a little place which had got stuck in the pointy bit of the horn. "You're some lucky" said God, "there's just this one place left. You can have that."

"That's some small for we," said Saint Dennis.

"Now, now, Saint Dennis," said God. "Dosn't ee go lookin a gift horse in the mouth. Ee's small right 'nough but ee's hansome. I thought that when I was creatin' of un. There's sea both sides an git cliffs and wild moorland te fill yer 'earts with wonder. But there's lots of little sheltered valleys so's you got places to go so you shaint be blawed away. And you shall have flowers all year round, golden gorse and campions and such. But just you wait until spring comes around an see what I got in store for ee."

"I s'pose size iden everything" said Saint Agnes. "What de ee think boys?"

"It de sound just like 'eaven" said Saint Ives and he was just turning round to say 'thanks very much' when he noticed it was just the boys and Saint Agnes again in the pub. God was nowhere to be seen. They rushed outside to catch a sight of Him and what they saw took their breath away. There were the rounded moorland hills with little wooded valleys between. The sea could be seen on both sides. And the light! And the flowers! And the magnificent carns! And the cliffs! And the rocky coves and sandy beaches! "Ee is 'eaven" said Saint Ives.

"Not quite boys" said Saint Agnes. "But ees 'ome."

Pilgrimage

Pilgrimage is less popular today than it once was but, who is to stop you making one if you are so moved? A recently retired minister of the church decided to make a tour of all the cathedrals in the British Isles. His plan was to start with Scotland, and then move down through the North of England until he arrived at Liverpool, which enjoys two cathedrals, one old and one new. He intended to cross the Irish Sea from Liverpool and visit the cathedrals in the North and the South of Ireland. This would allow him to take the ferry from Waterford to Milford Haven and then work his way, up through Wales before continuing his English tour, from North to South and then from East to West.

Towards the end of his trip the reverend gentleman had noticed an innovation. At the back of many of the cathedrals he visited was a golden telephone with a sign attached to it saying 'Direct Line to Heaven, £100 per minute'. In spite of the high price there was always a queue to use these phones.

The very last cathedral on his tour was the small, quite modern but still very beautiful Truro Cathedral. As he had come to expect, there, near the great doors, was the familiar golden phone with its sign 'Direct Line to Heaven, 10p per minute'. Astonished at the low price, the old priest sought out a cathedral guide and asked her why the cost was so much lower here than in all the other cathedrals he had visited.
"Ah!" said the guide, "that's because it's a local call."

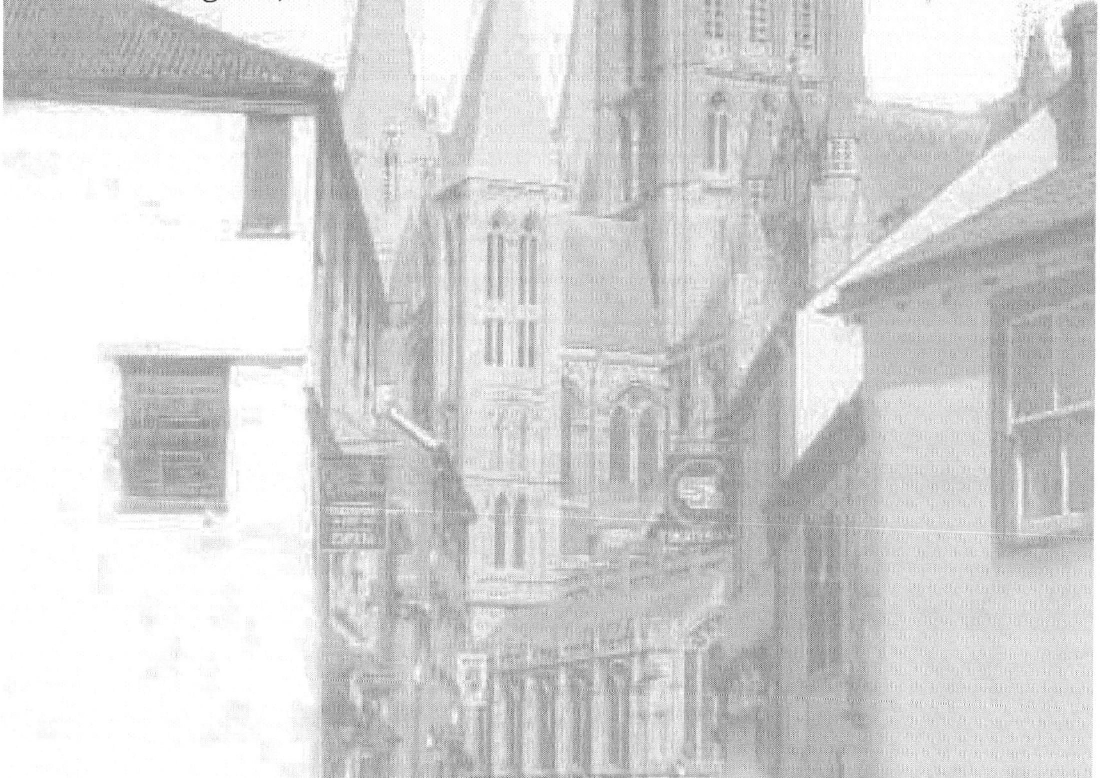